STUDY GUIDE TO ACCOMPANY

INVESTMENT
MANAGEMENT

R. Stephen Sears, Ph.D.
Texas Tech University
Gary L. Trennepohl, Ph.D.
Texas A & M University

Prepared by

Joseph D. Vu, Ph.D., CFA
DePaul University

D1451521

The Dryden Press
Harcourt Brace College Publishers

Fort Worth   Philadelphia   San Diego   New York   Orlando   Austin   San Antonio
Toronto   Montreal   London   Sydney   Tokyo

Address for Editorial Correspondence
The Dryden Press, 301 Commerce Street, Suite 3700, Fort Worth, TX 76102

Address for Orders
The Dryden Press, 6277 Sea Harbor Drive, Orlando, FL 32887
1-800-782-4479, or 1-800-433-0001 (in Florida)

ISBN: 0-03-030028-2

Printed in the United States of America

4 5 6 7 8 9 0 1 2 3   0 5 6   9 8 7 6 5 4 3 2 1

The Dryden Press
Harcourt Brace College Publishers

HOW TO USE THIS STUDY GUIDE

This study guide consists of twenty-two chapters that review the most important concepts of investment. The study guide is written as a supplement to the textbook *Investment Management* by Stephen Sears and Gary Trennepohl.

Each chapter of this study guide contains (1) an overview, (2) an outline, (3) vocabulary review, (4) definitional self-test questions, (5) conceptual self-test questions, (6) self-test problems, and (7) answers and solutions to the self-test questions and problems.

The overview gives you a general idea of what is contained in the chapter. The outline summarizes the chapter highlights in a concise, orderly form. The outline is intended to complement and not substitute for reading the textbook. You should read the textbook first and then read the chapter outline. The vocabulary review shows key words or concepts that you should understand.

The definitional self-test questions are designed to test your knowledge of the terms and concepts used in the chapter. After completing this section, you should score your results to make sure you understand the definitions thoroughly before moving to the conceptual questions.

The conceptual self-test questions are set in the true/false or multiple choice format, so that you can test yourself on key points in the chapter without the rigors of detailed calculation and presentation.

The self-test problems are written in a multiple choice format. They are designed to complement the numerical problems in your textbook. The answers and solutions to the self-test questions and problems are found at the end of each chapter.

I would like to thank Stephen Sears and Gary Trennepohl, the authors of the text *Investment Management,* for their encouragement. I have tried to make the study guide as clear and error-free as possible. Any comments and suggestions for improving the study guide would be appreciated. Suggestions should be sent to me at the address below.

Joseph D. Vu, CFA
Department of Finance
DePaul University
Chicago, Illinois 60604

CONTENTS

How to Use This Study Guide

CHAPTER 1

INVESTMENT MANAGEMENT: AN INTRODUCTION

AND OVERVIEW

OVERVIEW

This chapter provides an overview of investment management and gives you a better understanding of the following: (1) what an investment is and how investment decisions are influenced by the consumption patterns of individuals, (2) the components of an investment's rate of return and how risk can affect the investment process, (3) the concept of a probability distribution and how it can be used to measure a security's expected return and risk, (4) the four steps involved in investment, and (5) the concept of portfolio efficiency and the efficient frontier.

OUTLINE

I.   Investment allows individuals to change their consumption pattern in order to reach a higher level of wealth than is presently available.

    A.   Individuals should make consumption-investment decisions in a manner that will maximize their utility, where utility is a measure of the individual's level of satisfaction and will vary from one person to another.

    B.   We generally assume that individuals can maximize their utility by maximizing their wealth, where wealth is measured by the present value of the amount of money the individual has available to spend.

II. When making investment decisions, investors should consider three components of the required rate of return: (1) the real rate of interest, (2) the rate of expected inflation, and (3) the risk premium.

    A.   The real rate of interest represents the price borrowers pay, irrespective of the effects of other factors such as expected inflation and risk. The real rate of interest compensates a lender for the passage of time during which money is not available for current consumption. Borrowing or lending at this rate does not increase or decrease an individual's wealth, it merely represents the compensation required to shift the timing at which spending occurs.

B.   The rate of expected inflation represents the expected decline in purchasing power because prices may rise from the time an investment is made to the time when these investment dollars are spent. In addition to seeking compensation for the passage of time, investors also demand an additional return component as compensation for expected inflation.

C.   Risk deals with the uncertainty regarding the actual return on the investment and its impact on the future wealth of the investors.

In evaluating investments, investors should recognize that there are three elements in an investment's required rate of return.

$$\begin{array}{c} Required\ rate \\ of\ return \end{array} = \begin{array}{c} Real \\ rate \end{array} + \begin{array}{c} Expected \\ inflation \end{array} + \begin{array}{c} Risk \\ premium \end{array} \quad (1.1)$$

III.   The rate of return on an investment can be calculated as:

$$\begin{array}{c} Rate \\ of\ return \end{array} = \frac{\begin{array}{c}Ending\\price\end{array} + \begin{array}{c}Cash\\distributions\end{array} - \begin{array}{c}Beginning\\price\end{array}}{Beginning\ Price} \quad (1.2)$$

This rate of return is also called the holding period yield (HPY).

IV.   Investors should evaluate alternative investments in term of expected return and the measure of risk that captures the return uncertainty.

A.   The expected return, or the mean, is a weighted average of all possible returns, where the weights are the probabilities assigned to each return. The mean, or expected return value, is calculated as:

$$Mean = E(r_t) = \sum_{t=1}^{T} p_t r_t \quad (1.3)$$

B. Risk is typically measured by the standard deviation, which is the square root of the variance.

$$Variance = \sigma^2 = \sum_{t=1}^{T} p_t[r_t - E(r_t)]^2 \qquad (1.4)$$

$$Standard\ Deviation = \sigma = \sqrt{\sigma^2} \qquad (1.5)$$

V. Investors are generally assumed to be risk-averse. That is, they prefer less risk and holding expected return constant. Investors should choose investments to maximize their expected wealth or expected utility. Because each investor has an unique set of investment objectives, different investors will choose different investments.

VI. Investment management deals with the manner in which investors analyze, choose, and evaluate investments in terms of their risks and expected returns. An efficient market is a market in which investments that have higher expected returns also have higher levels of risk. In such a setting, one investment should not persistently dominate another in terms of risk and expected return. The management of investment portfolios can be divided into four steps:

A. Security analysis: develops and analyzes the probability return distributions and computes risk and expected return for each security.

B. Portfolio analysis helps to construct an optimal portfolio, which is defined as a portfolio that maximizes expected return for a given level of risk or minimizes risk for a given level of expected return. The set of optimal portfolios that provides the lowest level of risk at a given level of expected return is called the efficient frontier.

C. In portfolio selection, the efficient frontier is identified and then investors pick one portfolio that matches their preferences for expected return and risk.

D. In performance evaluation and revision, the chosen optimal portfolio should be evaluated periodically to determine if it still meets the risk and expected return objectives. If it does not, then a restructuring of the portfolio may be required.

VOCABULARY REVIEW

investment	standard deviation
utility	risk averse
real rate of interest	diversification
expected rate of inflation	investment management
risk	efficient market
risk premium	security analysis
holding period yield	optimal portfolio
probability distribution	efficient frontier
expected return	capital market line

SELF-TEST QUESTIONS

Definitional

1. The present value of an individual's income stream is called _____.

2. People can change their consumption-investment pattern by _____ and _____ .

3. _____ is a measure of individual's level of satisfaction.

4. Three components of an investment's required rate of return are the real rate of interest, the rate of expected inflation and the _____ _____ .

5. The uncertainty regarding the actual return on an investment is called _____ .

6. A _____ _____ is a mapping of all possible returns along with the probabilities associated with each return.

7. Most investors use the _____ _____ as a measure of risk using the same unit as the mean.

8. The rate of return on an investment is also called the _____ _____ _____ .

9. Investors who prefer less risk, holding expected return constant, are _____ _____ .

10. _____ means to invest in more than one asset.

11. A market in which investments that have higher expected returns also have higher levels of risk is called an _____ _____ .

12. A portfolio that maximizes expected return for a given level of risk is an _____ _____ .

13. The _____ _____ is the set of optimal portfolios that provides the lowest level of risk at a given level of expected return.

Conceptual

14. Investment can be defined as postponed consumption.

   a.   True   b.   False

15. Individuals can maximize their utility by maximizing their wealth.

   a.   True   b.   False

16. The required rate of return is equal to the real rate of interest plus the actual inflation rate.

   a.   True   b.   False

17. The holding period yield takes into consideration the security appreciation but not the cash distributions.

   a.   True   b.   False

18. The variance is the square root of the standard deviation.

   a.   True   b.   False

19. Investment A dominates investment B by providing a higher expected return and a somewhat higher risk.

   a.   True   b.   False

20. Security analysis deals with the manner in which investors analyze, choose, and evaluate investments in terms of their risk and expected return.

   a.   True   b.   False

21.   An optimal portfolio dominates all other portfolios at any level of risk and expected return.

    a.   True   b.   False

22.   Through diversification an investor can achieve a higher level of expected return at the same risk level afforded by individual investments.

    a.   True   b.   False

23.   Which of the following steps are necessary in investment management?

    a.   security analysis
    b.   portfolio analysis
    c.   portfolio selection
    d.   performance evaluation and revision
    e.   all of the above

24.   Which of the following statements is *most* correct?

    a.   Investment management uses the measure of risk and expected return to construct optimal portfolios.
    b.   Through diversification an investor can only achieve a higher level of expected return by taking more risk.
    c.   An optimal portfolio maximizes expected return for a given level of risk or minimizes risk for a given level of expected return.
    d.   All of the above statements are correct.

SELF-TEST PROBLEMS

1.   The stock of Illinois Power went from $18 to $21 last year. The stock paid dividend of $1. The rate of return of Illinois Power is

    a.   16.67 percent.
    b.   14.29 percent.
    c.   19.05 percent.
    d.   22.22 percent.
    e.   21.00 percent.

2. Assume the real rate of return rate is 3 percent, the expected rate of inflation is 5 percent, the actual rate of inflation is 6 percent, and the risk premium is 4.5 percent. The required rate of return is

    a. 8.0 percent.
    b. 12.5 percent.
    c. 18.5 percent.
    d. 13.5 percent.
    e. 14.0 percent.

    req = real + infl prem + risk prem

(The following data apply to Self-Test Problems 3 and 4.)

You are given the following return and probability information for Westinghouse and Goodyear stocks:

Westinghouse		Goodyear	
Return	Probability	Return	Probability
-6%	.20	4%	.10
2%	.40	7%	.40
10%	.30	10%	.40
25%	.10	14%	.10

3. The expected return and standard deviation of return for Westinghouse are

    a. 7.75 percent and 9.00 percent.
    b. 5.10 percent and 8.68 percent.
    c. 7.50 percent and 8.11 percent.
    d. 7.75 percent and 9.50 percent.
    e. none of the above

4. The expected return and standard deviation of return for Goodyear are

    a. 8.60 percent and 2.61 percent.
    b. 8.60 percent and 6.84 percent.
    c. 8.75 percent and 6.84 percent.
    d. 8.30 percent and 3.11 percent.
    e. none of the above

(The following data apply to Self-Test Problems 5 and 6.)

You are trying to decide which of the following common stocks to purchase; therefore, you collect the following information from the Value Line Investment Survey.

Company	Expected Return	Standard Deviation
Philadelphia Electric	8%	5%
Federal Express	7%	5%
Santa Fe Pacific	9%	8%
Alcoa	11%	12%
Caterpillar	10%	10%
Consolidated Edison	5%	6%
DuPont	12%	13%
McDonald's	14%	15%

5. The stock(s) that are dominated is/are

    a. Consolidated Edison.
    b. Federal Express and Philadelphia Electric.
    c. Consolidated Edison and Federal Express.
    d. Federal Express.
    e. McDonald's and Consolidated Edison.

6. If you are very risk-averse, the stock you should purchase is

    a. Consolidated Edison.
    b. Philadelphia Electric.
    c. Federal Express.
    d. Santa Fe Pacific.
    e. none of the above

ANSWERS TO SELF-TEST QUESTIONS

1.	wealth	13.	efficient frontier
2.	borrowing; lending	14.	True
3.	utility	15.	True
4.	risk premium	16.	False
5.	risk	17.	False
6.	probability distribution	18.	False
7.	standard deviation	19.	False
8.	holding period yield	20.	False
9.	risk averse	21.	False
10.	diversification	22.	True
11.	efficient market	23.	e
12.	optimal portfolio	24.	c

SOLUTIONS TO SELF-TEST PROBLEMS

1. c. The rate of return of Illinois Power stock is:

$$\frac{\$21 - \$18 + \$1}{\$21} = .1905 = 19.05\%$$

2. b. The required rate of return is:
3% + 5% + 4.5% = 12.5%

3. b. The expected return for Westinghouse is:
$$E(r) = (-6\%)(.2) + (2\%)(.4) + (10\%)(.3) + (25\%)(.1)$$
$$= -1.2\% + 0.8\% + 3.0\% + 2.5\%$$
$$= 5.1\%$$

The variance of return for Westinghouse is:
$$\sigma^2(r) = (-6-5.1)^2(.2) + (2-5.1)^2(.4) + (10-5.1)^2(.3)$$
$$+ (25-5.1)^2(.1)$$
$$= 24.64 + 3.84 + 7.20 + 39.60$$
$$= 75.28$$

The standard deviation of return is the square root of 75.28 which is 8.68 percent.

4. a. The expected return for Goodyear is:
    $E(r)$ $= (4\%)(.1) + (7\%)(.4) + (10\%)(.4) + (14\%)(.1)$
    $= 0.4\% + 2.8\% + 4.0\% + 1.4\%$
    $= 8.6\%$

    The variance of return for Goodyear is:
    $\sigma^2(r) = (4-8.6)^2(.1) + (7-8.6)^2(.4) + (10-8.6)^2(.4)$
    $+ (14-8.6)^2(.1)$
    $= 2.12 + 1.02 + 0.78 + 2.92$
    $= 6.84$

    The standard deviation of return is the square root of 6.84 which is 2.61 percent.

5. c. Both Consolidated Edison and Federal Express stocks are dominated by the Philadelphia Electric stock because they have lower expected return and higher or the same standard deviation of return relative to the Philadelphia Electric stock.

6. b. If you are very risk-averse, you should buy the Philadelphia Electric stock because it is a non-dominated stock with the lowest standard deviation of return.

CHAPTER 2

ALTERNATIVE FINANCIAL SECURITIES

OVERVIEW

This chapter provides a brief description of the following financial securities: (1) fixed-income securities, (2) common stocks, (3) preferred stocks, (4) foreign securities, (5) options, (6) futures contracts, and (7) investment company shares. In addition, this chapter discusses recent innovations in security development and tax considerations for investments.

OUTLINE

I.   Investment can be classified into two types: real and financial. A real asset is a physical commodity or a tangible asset. A financial asset represents a monetary claim on a real asset. Financial securities have two desirable features: liquidity and widely available information on their returns.

II.   Fixed-income securities have three general features: (1) their prices are quoted in yield to maturity, (2) they have a specified maturity date, and (3) they have a fixed schedule for the repayment of principal and interest.

   A.   Demand deposits and time deposits.

      1.   Checking accounts are interest-bearing checking accounts offered by financial institutions such as commercial banks, savings and loans, and credit unions. Checking accounts are called demand deposits because money in these accounts can be withdrawn on demand.
      2.   Savings accounts are interest-bearing accounts which may impose a penalty if money is withdrawn early.
      3.   Certificates of deposit (CDs) are time deposits that have a fixed maturity date. The interest earned is higher than that of passbook savings accounts.
      4.   Money market investment CDs require a minimum balance of $10,000, carry a minimum maturity of six months, and earn interest at least 0.25 percent above the rate for a Treasury bill of the same maturity.

5.   Indexed CDs returns are indexed to the performance of the stock market.

6.   Eurodollar deposits are dollar-denominated deposits held in a commercial bank outside of the United States.

B.   Money market securities are short-term debt instruments that have very low risk of default, high level of liquidity, and are usually sold at a discount from their principal value.

     1.   Treasury bills are issued on a discount basis by the U.S Treasury with maturities of 13 weeks, 26 weeks and 52 weeks. Interest earned on Treasury bills is exempt from state and local taxes. Prices and yields from Treasury bills are reported on the bank discount yield basis which uses a 360-day year in the computation.

     2.   Commercial paper is a short-term, unsecured promissory note issued by only the largest and the most financially secured firms. Commercial paper can be sold either on a discount basis or as an interest-bearing note.

     3.   A banker's acceptance is a promissory note which the accepting bank agrees to pay at a future date. Banker's acceptances are short-term notes that are issued at a discount.

     4.   A negotiable CD is a deposit for which the depositor can negotiate the rate and term to maturity with the borrowing institution. Negotiable CDs are issued in denominations of at least $100,000 and carry a maturity of at least 14 days.

     5.   A Eurodollar CD is a large certificate, in excess of $100,000, that represents a dollar-denominated deposit held in a bank outside of the United States.

     6.   A repurchase agreement is a contract between a seller and a buyer whereby the seller agrees to repurchase U.S. government securities at an agreed-upon price and at a stated time in the future.

C.   Bonds are fixed-income investments for which the issuer promises to pay a fixed amount of interest periodically and to repay the principal at maturity.

     1.   Treasury issues—Treasury notes are U.S. government bonds with maturities ranging from one to ten years. Treasury bonds are long-term government bonds with maturities ranging from 10 to 30 years. Prices for Treasury notes and bonds are quoted in thirty-seconds per $1,000 of par value. The Treasury also issues two types of savings bonds. Series EE savings bonds are discount bonds, where the interest accrues over time and is payable at maturity or when sold. Series HH bonds carry an original maturity of 10 years and pay interest semiannually. Series HH bonds are available only in an exchange for Series EE bonds that have been held for at least six months.

2. Federal agencies' bonds come in a variety of forms and maturities. Some are short-term, discounted notes. However, most are interest-bearing bonds with maturity ranging to 40 years. Since 1986, all new agency issues are in book-entry form.

3. Municipal bonds are promissory notes issued by a state or local government. There are two types of municipal bonds: general obligation bonds, which are backed by the issuer's taxing authority, and revenue bonds, which are backed only by the revenues of a project such as a toll road. The interest income of municipal bonds is tax-exempt at the federal level and in general not subject to state and local taxes in the state where the municipal bond is issued. The taxable equivalent yield for a tax-exempt municipal bond is given by the following equation:

$$\text{Taxable yield equivalent for a municipal bond} = \frac{\text{Municipal bond yield}}{1 - \text{Investor's marginal tax rate}} \qquad (2.4)$$

4. Corporate bonds, long-term debt issued by corporations, promise to pay interest at a specified rate plus the principal at maturity. They are generally issued in denominations of $1,000 and normally pay interest semiannually.

5. Types of corporate bonds—Corporate bonds are distinguished from each other by the type of protection given to bondholders. Secured bonds include mortgage bonds, which are collateralized by fixed assets of the corporation, and collateral trust bonds, which are backed by financial assets. Unsecured bonds such as debentures and subordinated debentures have no collateral and are backed only by the ability of the firm to pay.

6. Specialty bonds are bonds whose payment characteristics differ from the typical bond. A zero-coupon bond is a bond that pays no interest or coupons. These bonds are sold at a deep discount from their par value. A mortgage-backed pass-through security is a bond collateralized by a pool of mortgages underlying the security. Collateralized mortgage obligations (CMOs) are similar to pass-through securities, except security holders are classified according to how principal repayments are handled. CMOs divide security holders into various classes called tranches. Owners of securities in the first tranche receive all the prepayments until their security interests are paid in full. Then security holders of the second tranche begin receiving all payments, and so on until security holders in the last tranche are paid off.

7. International bonds are classified into two groups: bonds denominated in U.S. dollars and bonds denominated in other currencies. The U.S.-dollar-denominated bonds include Eurodollar and Yankee bonds.

III. Corporate stocks

    A. Preferred stock is a hybrid security because in some ways it resembles a bond and in other way it resembles common stock. Similar to bonds, most preferred stock dividends are fixed and do not change through time. Similar to common stock, preferred stock is treated as equity and has no maturity date. Preferred stockholders have priority over common stockholders in receiving dividends and also in the event of the company's bankruptcy.

    B. Common stocks represent ownership in the corporations. Common stockholders have voting rights to elect officers and directors, and usually, preemptive rights that give them the first right of refusal on any new common stock offerings.

    C. International stocks have grown rapidly in the last decade, especially in Europe and in the Pacific area. Investors should be careful with direct investment in foreign stocks, since their prices are subject to political risk and changing exchange rates.

IV. A derivative security is an instrument whose value is primarily dependent on the value of another security. A warrant is a derivative security that gives the holder the right to buy a stated number of shares of common stock at the exercise price over the life of the warrant (usually two years or more). A call option gives its holder the right to buy a certain amount of an asset at a specific price over a period of time. A put option gives the holder the right to sell a certain amount of an asset at the exercise price over a period of time. A futures contract is a commitment to buy or sell a given quantity of an asset for a specified price at a predetermined time.

V. Investment company shares come in two types: closed-end and open-end. A closed-end company issues a fixed number of shares and uses the proceeds to invest in other financial securities. The company neither repurchases outstanding shares from the general public nor issues further shares. The share price of a closed-end fund can trade above or below the net asset value (NAV), which is the total market value of all securities held in the fund, divided by the number of shares outstanding. An open-end fund, or a mutual fund, is a portfolio of securities for which shares continue to be bought and sold by the issuer after the initial public offering.

VI. Recent trends and new security developments include the move toward a certificateless market, the globalization of investment markets, the securitization and guaranteeing of new securities, and the creation of complex securities, such as puttable bonds, and Salomon Brothers S&P 500 indexed notes.

VOCABULARY REVIEW

real asset
financial asset
liquidity
yield to maturity
demand deposit
time deposit
certificate of deposit
eurodollar deposit
money market security
treasury bill
commercial paper
banker's acceptance
negotiable CD
repurchase agreement
Treasury note
Treasury bond
book-entry security
municipal bond
securitization

revenue bond
general obligation bond
sinking fund
mortgage bond
collateral trust bond
debenture
junk bond
mortgage-backed pass-through
  security
collateralized mortgage obligation
Yankee bond
preemptive right
derivative security
warrant
net asset value
closed-end fund
open-end fund
American depository receipt

SELF-TEST QUESTIONS

Definitional

1. A claim in money terms on some economic entity is called a _____ _____ .

2. _____ measures the ability to sell a security quickly at a price that is readily determined.

3. The expected annualized return to the investor of a fixed-income security is called _____ _____ _____ .

4. Investors who seek higher yields can invest in a _____ _____ which is a dollar-denominated deposit that is held in a commercial bank outside the United States.

5. Short term, risk-free securities issued by the U.S. Treasury are called _____ _____ .

6.   _____ _____ is a short-term, unsecured promissory note issued by large and financially secure firms.

7.   A long-term promissory note issued by a state or local government is called a _____ _____ .

8.   _____ are unsecured corporate bonds which are backed only by the ability of the firm to pay back the interest and principal.

9.   A bond that pays no interest and is sold at a deep discount from par value is called a _____ _____ _____ .

10. A _____ _____ _____ _____ is a security collateralized by a pool of mortgages.

11. _____ and _____ bonds are examples of U.S.-dollar-denominated foreign bonds.

12. Many firms provide their stockholders with a _____ _____ , which gives them the first right of refusal on any new common stock offerings.

13. A _____ _____ gives its holder the right to sell a certain amount of an asset for a specific price over a period of time.

14. A commitment to buy or sell a given quantity of an asset for a specified price at a predetermined time is called a _____ _____ _____ .

15. An investment company that neither repurchases the outstanding shares nor sells additional shares to the general public is called a _____ _____ _____ .

16. An _____ _____ _____ is a domestically traded security that represents a claim to shares of foreign stocks.

Conceptual

17. A financial asset can include a tangible asset such as land or a building.

        a.   True   b.   False

18. A real asset is typically more liquid than a financial asset.

        a.   True   b.   False

19. A money market security has very little risk of default because it is insured by the Federal Deposit Insurance Corporation (FDIC).

    a.   True   b.   False

20. The interest income from Treasury securities is exempt from state and local taxes.

    a.   True   b.   False

21. Commercial paper is risk-free because it is issued by only the largest and most financially secure firms.

    a.   True   b.   False

22. Both Series EE and HH bonds are issued by the U.S. Treasury and, therefore, have virtually no default risk.

    a.   True   b.   False

23. The interest income of all Federal agency bonds is exempt from state and local taxes.

    a.   True   b.   False

24. A general obligation bond has lower risk than a revenue bond because the state or local government can raise taxes to repay the debt.

    a.   True   b.   False

25. The yield on a municipal bond must be higher than that of a Treasury security with the same maturity because the Treasury security is risk-free.

    a.   True   b.   False

26. Investors who buy collateralized mortgage obligations have less principal prepayment problems than those who invest in mortgage-backed pass-through securities.

    a.   True   . b.   False

27. Which of the following statements is most correct?

a. Eurodollar deposits can include Eurodollar bonds and Yankee bonds.
b. Eurodollar deposits are dollar-denominated deposits held in a commercial bank outside the United States.
c. Eurodollar deposits are insured up to $100,000 by the Federal Deposit Insurance Corporation (FDIC).
d. Eurodollar deposits pay about the same yield as U.S. time deposits.
e. All the above statements are correct.

28. The advantage of preferred stocks relative to common stocks is

a. preferred stock dividends are always cumulative.
b. preferred stocks cannot be called or repurchased.
c. preferred stockholders receive their dividends ahead of common stockholders.
d. preferred stockholders receive more than one vote per share.
e. all of the above

29. Common stocks can be classified along business lines, such as

a. transportation firms.
b. industrial firms.
c. public utilities.
d. financial firms.
e. all of the above

30. Compared to call options, warrants

a. have longer maturities.
b. pay dividends, just like common stocks.
c. carry voting rights.
d. are always traded over the counter.
e. none of the above

31. Which of the following statements is *most* correct?

a. A mutual fund *always* buys and sells shares at the net asset value.
b. A closed-end fund's shares can trade at a premium or discount from the net asset value.
c. A closed-end company cannot convert to an open-end company.
d. There are more stocks traded on the New York Stock Exchange than the number of mutual funds in the United States.
e. All of the above statements are correct.

SELF-TEST PROBLEMS

1. An investor who is in the 28% tax bracket buys a municipal bond with a yield of 5.9%. What is the taxable yield equivalent for this municipal bond?

    a. 8.55%
    b. 5.90%
    c. 8.19%
    d. 21.07%
    e. 8.81%

2. A zero coupon bond with a par value of $1000 is currently selling at $690. The bond will mature in 5 years. What is the annual compound yield to maturity of this zero coupon bond?

    a. 8.61%
    b. 7.70%
    c. 6.90%
    d. 14.50%
    e. 7.50%

3. A $10,000 Treasury bill with 60 days to maturity is selling at a discount of 3.40 percent. What is the market price of this Treasury bill?

    a. $9,937.53
    b. $9,929.60
    c. $9,956.67
    d. $9,943.33
    e. $9,940.28

4. Cecilia Jackson is thinking about buying fixed-income securities but she is concerned about the effect of taxes on the interest income she receives. Currently her marginal federal income tax bracket is 28 percent and her marginal state income tax bracket is 4 percent. Of the following bonds, which one will result in the highest return after federal and state income taxes for Cecilia? Assume that all five bonds are priced at the par value of $1,000 and that Cecilia plans to hold the bond until maturity.

    a. One year, 7.5% AT&T bond   5.1
    b. One year, 7.0% U.S. Treasury bond   5.04
    c. One year, 5.25% out-of-state municipal bond   5.04
    d. One year, 5.0% in-state municipal bond   5
    e. One year, 6.9% U.S. Treasury note   4.968

5.   Which of the following zero-coupon corporate bonds have the highest annual compound yield to maturity?

a.   AT&T bond selling at $710 with 6 years to maturity   *5.8*
b.   IBM bond selling at $540 with 9 years to maturity   *7.08*
c.   Chrysler bond selling at $500 with 11 years to maturity   *6.5*
d.   Commonwealth Edison bond selling at $400 with 20 years to maturity   *4.1*
e.   American Express bond selling at $820 with 4 years to maturity   *5*

6.   The dollar value of the U.S. Treasury bond quoted at 108–26 is

a. $1,082.60.
b. $1,088.13.
c. $1,080.81.
d. $1,084.06.
e.   none of the above

ANSWERS TO SELF-TEST QUESTIONS

1.	financial asset	17.	False
2.	liquidity	18.	False
3.	yield to maturity	19.	False
4.	Eurodollar deposit	20.	True
5.	Treasury bills	21.	False
6.	commercial paper	22.	True
7.	municipal bond	23.	False
8.	debentures	24.	True
9.	zero coupon bond	25.	False
10.	mortgage-backed pass-through security	26.	True
		27.	b
11.	Eurodollar, Yankee	28.	c
12.	preemptive right	29.	e
13.	put option	30.	a
14.	futures contract	31.	b
15.	closed-end company		
16.	American Depository Receipt		

SOLUTIONS TO SELF-TEST PROBLEMS

1.   c.   The taxable yield equivalent for this municipal bond is:
$$(5.9\%)/(1 - 0.28) = 8.19\%$$

2.   b.   The annual compound yield to maturity of this zero coupon bond is:
$$(\$1,000/\$690)^{1/5} - 1 = 7.70\%$$

3.   d.   The dollar discount from face value is calculated first:
$$\$10,000 \times .034 \times (60/360) = \$56.67$$
The market price of this Treasury bill is:
$$\$10,000 - \$56.67 = \$9,943.33$$

4.   a.   The AT&T bond has the highest return after federal and state income taxes for Cecilia.
The after-tax rate of return for holding the AT&T bond is:
$$7.5\%(1 - 0.32) = 5.10\%$$
The after-tax rate of return for holding the U.S. Treasury bond is:
$$7.0\%(1 - 0.28) = 5.04\%$$
The after-tax rate of return for holding the out-of-state municipal bond is:
$$5.25\%(1 - 0.04) = 5.04\%$$
The after-tax rate of return for holding the in-state municipal bond is 5.0 percent because the interest is tax exempt at both the federal and state levels.
The after-tax rate of return for holding the U.S. Treasury note is:
$$6.9\%(1 - 0.28) = 4.97\%$$

5.   b.   The IBM bond has the highest annual compound yield to maturity of 7.09 percent.
The annual compound yield to maturity for the AT&T bond is:

$$\left[\frac{1,000}{710}\right]^{1/6} - 1 = 5.87\%$$

The annual compound yield to maturity for the IBM bond is:

$$\left[\frac{1,000}{540}\right]^{1/9} - 1 = 7.09\%$$

The annual compound yield to maturity for the Chrysler bond is:

$$\left[\frac{1,000}{500} \right]^{1/11} - 1 = 6.5\%$$

The annual compound yield to maturity for the Commonwealth Edison bond is:

$$\left[\frac{1,000}{400} \right]^{1/20} - 1 = 4.69\%$$

The annual compound yield to maturity for the American Express bond is:

$$\left[\frac{1,000}{820} \right]^{1/4} - 1 = 5.09\%$$

6.   b.   Prices for Treasury bonds are quoted in thirty-seconds per $1,000 of par value. Thus 108–26 translates into 108 and 26/32 or $1,088.13.

CHAPTER 3

THE ORGANIZATION AND FUNCTIONING

OF FINANCIAL MARKETS

OVERVIEW

This chapter describes the characteristics and functions of financial markets and gives you a better understanding of the following: (1) how new securities are brought to the market, (2) the functions of the secondary market and how trading is done for various securities, (3) how margin and short selling are used in trading securities, and (4) the characteristics and organization of the exchanges for stocks, bonds, options, and futures.

OUTLINE

I. The primary function of financial markets is to facilitate the transfer of funds between those who have excess funds and those who need funds. The second function of financial markets is financial product innovation, such as bundling and unbundling earning components of assets to meet the objectives of investors.

II. In an efficient market prices fully and instantaneously reflect all available information. External efficiency means buyers and sellers will trade securities at prices reflecting a fair or equilibrium price, whereas internal efficiency implies transaction costs and taxes are low enough so as not to distort the impact of new information on security prices.

III. The primary market allows the original issuers of securities to sell directly to investors, usually with the help of investment banks.

   A. Private placement or public offering—Under private placement, the securities are sold directly to one large investor or a small number of individuals, typically less than 36 investors. Firms that use public offerings must register their securities with the Securities and Exchange Commission (SEC).

   B. Registration of securities—Both initial public offerings (sale of a firm's common stock to the public for the first time) and seasoned offerings require registration with the SEC and the states where the securities will be sold. At the same time of registration, the firm distributes a red herring or preliminary prospectus to prospective investors. After the registration statement is accepted by the SEC, the firm prints the prospectus, which must be provided to all buyers of the new offering. Since 1982, the SEC permits shelf registration, which allows a company to keep the registration authorization on the shelf up to two years to issue the securities.

C. Typically, six functions are attributable to investment bankers in primary market offerings.

1. Originating the security issue and providing advice and counseling to issuing firms.
2. Underwriting (transfer of risk from the issuer to the investment bank). Under the firm commitment, the investment bank buys the entire issue from the firm for resale to the public. In the best-effort arrangement, the investment bank acts as an agent making the best effort to sell the securities to the public. Any unsold securities are returned to the issuer. In the all-or-none arrangement, the investment bank must sell the entire issue during a period at a specified price. If sufficient shares are not sold, the issue is canceled and the buyers' checks are returned. In the standby agreement, which is used only in conjunction with the rights offering, the investment bank purchases all the unexercised rights and subscribes to the new issue by exercising the rights.
3. Forming a syndicate consisting of other investment banks to help in the sale and distribution of the new securities.
4. Distributing the securities to the public—Two weeks before offering date, the maximum price for the securities must be announced. The actual offering price is not established until immediately before the offering date. The investment bank and the selling group are prohibited from selling the security at a price different from the offering price.
5. Stabilizing the security's market price—The SEC allows the lead underwriter to buy stock in the secondary market to maintain the price of the stock.
6. Developing a secondary market for the issue.

D. New issues and the price behavior of common stock: existing common stock prices of initial public offerings appear to be consistently underpriced from 10 percent to 52 percent. However, the period of underpricing is short-lived, lasting about one to four weeks; after price stabilization occurs, the stock prices of initial public offerings follow the random pattern exhibited by seasoned securities.

IV. The secondary market involves the trade of a security between two parties neither of whom is the issuer of the security.

 A. Functions of secondary markets—The primary function of the secondary market is to provide liquidity. Liquidity is the ability to buy or sell a security quickly at a price reflecting its economic worth. Another function of a secondary market is to provide price discovery to investors.

 B. The trading process on organized exchanges.

  1. To be eligible to trade on an exchange floor, it is necessary to buy a membership or a seat. When buying a seat, members register with the exchange according to the function they intend to perform. Commission brokers execute transactions for public orders that originate off the exchange floor. Floor brokers are independent brokers who handle trade for other brokers too busy to handle all their trades. Floor traders are investors who buy and sell securities for their own accounts. Specialists perform the roles of broker, dealer, and auctioneer for the exchange. Each stock is assigned to a specialist. As a dealer, specialists maintain a book of limit orders, which are orders to buy or sell at a price away from current market quotes. As an auctioneer, specialists set opening prices each day to clear accumulated market orders.

  2. Order specifications—Investors can specify a variety of orders. A buy order is an instruction to buy a security. A sell order is an instruction to sell a security that you own. A sell-short order is an order to sell a stock that you do not own, which will result in a profit if the stock falls in price.

  3. Margin transactions represent the purchase of shares using credit. The initial margin required is 50 percent of the purchase price. Maintenance margin, which is the level of equity that must be maintained in the account, is currently 25 percent of the account's market value for long positions and 30 percent for short positions.

 C. The organized exchanges.

  1. The New York Stock Exchange (NYSE) is organized as a not-for-profit organization to provide a facility for members to buy and sell securities. There are 1,408 members of the NYSE. At the end of 1990, there were 2,284 issues of common and preferred stocks listed on the NYSE. To be eligible for trading on the NYSE, the firm must apply to the exchange and must meet its listing requirements.

2. The American Stock Exchange (AMEX) is much smaller than the NYSE, and is also a New York state not-for-profit corporation. The AMEX lists a variety of securities including U.S. and foreign stocks, options, warrants, corporate and U.S. government bonds. Like the NYSE, the AMEX uses a specialist system to facilitate trading.

3. The Over-the-counter market (OTC) is the largest secondary market in terms of number of issues traded. The OTC is not a physical location where members come to trade. It is a collection of market makers who provide firm price quotes on securities they buy or sell for their own account. In 1971, the National Association of Security Dealers Automatic Quotations (NASDAQ) system was implemented to provide electronic, real-time quotes for major OTC stocks. In addition, the National Market System (NMS) contains a subset of NASDAQ securities on which real-time transaction prices, trading volume, and high, low and closing prices are available.

4. Regional exchanges are stock exchanges not located in New York City. These exchanges list stocks of small companies that are of interest to local investors, and some stocks that are also listed on the NYSE or AMEX.

5. Foreign exchanges—The major foreign exchanges are the Tokyo, London, and German exchanges. Many foreign stocks are traded on the U.S. exchanges and in the OTC market in the form of American depository receipts (ADRs), which are denominated in U.S. dollars.

V. The options and futures exchanges—The primary market for options is the Chicago Board of Options Exchange (CBOE) and the primary futures market is the Chicago Board of Trade (CBOT). Trading in options and futures is based on an open auction market in which bids and offers are made by open outcry in a designated trading pit. Participants in the pit include market makers, who buy and sell for their own accounts and floor brokers, who execute customer orders for their firms.

VOCABULARY REVIEW

efficient capital market
primary market
private placement
Securities and exchange commission
initial public offering
red herring prospectus
shelf registration
letter stock
underwriting
secondary market
bid-asked spread
specialist
floor broker
American depository receipt

sell short
up-tick rule
open order
stop order
margin transaction
hypothecation
margin call
marked to market
market maker
NASDAQ
third market
fourth market
limit order

SELF-TEST QUESTIONS

Definitional

1. A market in which security prices fully reflect all available information is called an _____ _____ _____ .

2. A _____ _____ trade occurs when the original issuer of a security sells it to an investor.

3. The sale of a firm's common stock to the public for the first time is called an

    _____ _____ _____ .

4. The arrangement in which the underwriter agrees to buy the entire new issue from the firm for resale to the public is called a _____ _____ .

5. A _____ _____ trade involves the exchange of a security between two parties neither of whom is the issuer of the security.

6. An independent broker who handles trades for other brokers who are too busy to handle all their business is called a _____ _____ .

7. A NYSE member who performs the roles of a broker, dealer, and auctioneer for the exchange is called a _____ .

8. A _____ _____ order is an order to sell a security that the investor does not own.

9. The rule that prevents investors from selling short a stock when its price is falling is called the _____ _____ rule.

10. The act of pledging securities as collateral for a loan is called _____.

11. A _____ _____ is a trade involving 10,000 or more shares of a single security.

12. A _____ _____ is a dealer who regularly buys and sells a particular security.

13. The direct trading of securities between investors without any help of brokers is called the _____ _____ trade.

14. _____ _____ _____ represent ownership of foreign companies traded on the U.S. exchanges and in the OTC market.

Conceptual

15. The primary function of the financial markets is financial product innovation.

a. True   b. False

16. In an efficient market, security prices fully and instantaneously reflect all available information.

a. True   b. False

17. Depth refers to a market that can handle changes in the volume offered for purchases or sales with minimum distortion in the security's price.

a. True   b. False

18. A primary market trade is the exchange of a currently existing security between two investors.

a. True   b. False

19. Shelf registration allows a company to keep the SEC registration authorization on the shelf indefinitely until the time is right to bring the issue to market.

    a.   True   b.   False

20. Securities issued by the U.S. government, states, and municipalities are exempt from registration with the SEC.

    a.   True   b.   False

21. Existing common stock of firms that issue new common stock tend to rise when the market learns of pending issue.

    a.   True   b.   False

22. In an initial public offering, best-effort issues are usually more underpriced than firm-commitment issues.

    a.   True   b.   False

23. Because initial public offerings are underpriced on average, buying and holding these stocks will generate excess returns to the purchasers.

    a.   True   b.   False

24. The organized exchanges, such as the New York Stock Exchange, buy and sell securities and set their prices.

    a.   True   b.   False

25. A floor broker executes transactions for public orders that originate off the exchange floor.

    a.   True   b.   False

26. For the New York Stock Exchange, no stock is assigned to more than one specialist.

    a.   True   b.   False

27. Short selling a security does not require any margin or collateral.

    a.   True   b.   False

28. A good-till-canceled order remains in the book of the specialist indefinitely until it is canceled by the investor.

   a.   True   b.   False

29. Listing a security on the NYSE precludes a firm from listing the same security on a different exchange.

   a.   True   b.   False

30. An American depository receipt is sponsored if the foreign issuer agrees to comply with all SEC reporting requirements.

   a.   True   b.   False

31. Investment bankers typically provide the following functions:

   a. originating the security issue
   b. underwriting
   c. distributing the security to the public
   d. stabilizing the security's market price
   e. all of the above

32. Which of the following statements is *most* correct?

   a.   Before selling to the public, all securities must be registered with the SEC.
   b.   The preliminary prospectus must include complete financial statements and the actual offering price of the security.
   c.   Most initial public offerings typically are underpriced.
   d.   Securities issued under shelf registration rules account for more than half of all new security offerings.
   e.   All of the above statements are correct.

33. Which of the following statements is *most* correct?

   a.   Because a specialist is given the monopoly power to make a market on a particular stock, all trades must pass through the specialist.
   b.   The New York Stock Exchange rules require specialists to maintain a fair and orderly market in their stocks.
   c.   Most specialists only earn a fair rate of return on their capital because the stock market is efficient.
   d.   A specialist can also perform the function of a commission broker.
   e.   Each of the above statements is false.

SELF-TEST PROBLEMS

(The following data apply to Self-Test Problems 1 to 4.)

Daniel Johnson just opened a margin account with Merrill Lynch. This firm has a policy of 50 percent initial margin and 30 percent maintenance margin. Daniel bought 200 shares of IBM at $80 per share on margin.

1. To what price may the IBM stock decline before Daniel gets a margin call?

    a. $40.00
    b. $56.08
    c. $57.14
    d. $24.02
    e. $52.55

2. If IBM stock suddenly falls to $50 per share, how much cash must Daniel deposit to his account to satisfy maintenance margin?

    a. $1,428
    b. $589
    c. $1,000
    d. $561
    e. $679

3. If IBM stock rises to $90 per share, Daniel's equity balance in the account is

    a. $8,000.
    b. $10,000.
    c. $18,000.
    d. $9,000.
    e. none of the above

4. If the maintenance margin is raised to 35 percent, to what price may the IBM stock fall before Daniel gets a margin call?

    a. $52.00
    b. $57.14
    c. $61.54
    d. $53.33
    e. none of the above

31

5.   You want to sell short Syntex stock and the last trade was $24.75. You place an order with your broker at Pacific Brokerage Service to short the stock at the next possible price. The responses below represent the dollar-price sequence for Syntex after you place your order. At which price will your short sale be executed?

a. $24.63
b. $24.50
c. $24.50
d. $24.75
e. $24.88

ANSWERS TO SELF-TEST QUESTIONS

1.	efficient capital market	18.	False
2.	primary market	19.	False
3.	initial public offering	20.	True
4.	firm commitment	21.	False
5.	secondary market	22.	True
6.	floor broker	23.	False
7.	specialist	24.	False
8.	sell short	25.	False
9.	up-tick	26.	True
10.	hypothecation	27.	False
11.	block trade	28.	False
12.	market maker	29.	False
13.	fourth market	30.	True
14.	American depository receipts	31.	e
15.	False	32.	c
16.	True	33.	b
17.	False		

SOLUTIONS TO SELF-TEST PROBLEMS

1. c. Total investment (TI) = 200 x $80 = $16,000
        Loan (D)   = 50% x $16,000 = $8,000
        Equity (E)   = $16,000 – $8,000 = $8,000
        Let P be the price of IBM that will cause a margin call.
                $0.3 = E/TI = (TI - D)/TI = 1 - \$8,000/(200)(P)$
        Solving this equation, $P = \$57.14$
        Daniel will get a margin call when IBM stock price declines to $57.14.

2. a. The additional money that Daniel must deposit is:

$$0.3 = \frac{Equity}{TI} = \frac{[(200)(\$50) - \$8,000] + new\ money}{(200)(\$50) + new\ money}$$

Solving this equation, new money = $1,428.57

3. b. If IBM rises to $90 per share, the total value of Daniel's investment is $90 x 200 = $18,000. The outstanding loan is still $8,000. Therefore, Daniel's equity balance is $10,000.

4. c. Let P be the price of IBM that will cause a margin call.
        $0.35 = E/TI = (TI - D)/TI = 1 - [\$8,000/(200)(P)]$
        Solving this equation, $P = \$61.54$
        With a new maintenance margin of 35 percent, Daniel will get a margin call when IBM stock price declines to $61.54.

5. d. The short sale can only be executed at an up-tick or at a zero-plus (unchanged stock price following an up-tick). Therefore, your short sale will be executed at $24.75.

CHAPTER 4

MARKET INDICATORS, AVERAGES,

AND INDEXES

OVERVIEW

This chapter illustrates the following: (1) the use of market indicators and indexes, (2) how the Dow Jones averages are calculated, (3) how value-weighted indexes such as the S&P 500, NYSE, and NASDAQ are calculated, (4) indexes on foreign exchanges, (5) bond market indexes, (6) indexes underlying options and futures contracts, and (7) the advantages and disadvantages of using indexes as market indicators.

OUTLINE

I.   Because security prices tend to move together, market indexes can successfully indicate the price performance of stocks and bonds. Market indexes are used to provide a general indicator of the market's performance, to serve as a benchmark to measure the performance of investment managers, to serve as an underlying asset for index futures and option contracts, and to serve as an indicator of future economic activity.

II.   Stock market indicators and their differences—Market averages are calculated by adding together the prices of the component stocks and dividing by the specified divisor. Market indexes compare the current level of component securities' prices or market values with a base period value.

III. Dow Jones Averages.

    A.   Composition—The Dow Jones averages consist of the Dow Jones Industrial Average (DJIA), Transportation Average, Utility Average, and the Dow Jones Composite, which is an aggregate of the other three. The 30 stocks in the Industrial Average are all large, well-known industrial corporations. The Transportation Average is composed of 20 transportation stocks, including airlines, railroads, and trucking companies. The Utility Average has 15 utility companies.

    B.   Method of calculation—The DJIA is calculated by totaling the price of 30 stocks and dividing by the current divisor. The divisor in 1928 was 30, but stock splits and stock dividends require the adjustment of the divisor through time. In

December 1991, the divisor was 0.559. The DJIA is a price-weighted average. The higher the stock price, the greater its effect on the DJIA calculation.

C. Evaluation—To the general public, the Dow Jones averages are the most familiar stock market indicators. However, these averages are seldom used as benchmark measures for investment managers because the DJIA only includes 30 blue-chip stocks and is a priced-weighted average that does not consider the market value of each component stock. Moreover, biases in the construction of the DJIA make it impossible to compare its values accurately through time.

IV. Standard and Poor's (S&P) indexes—The S&P 500 Composite Index consists of 400 industrial stocks, 20 transportation stocks, 40 utility stocks, and 40 financial stocks. The S&P Midcap series includes 400 stocks. Firms in the S&P indexes are predominantly well-known NYSE firms. All of the S&P indexes are value-weighted. The S&P 500 is widely used as a benchmark performance measure for professional managers.

V. New York Stock Exchanges indexes—There are five NYSE indexes: the Composite Index includes all NYSE stocks, the Industrial index, the Transportation index, the Utility index, and the Finance index. All the NYSE indexes are market-value weighted and are calculated in the same manner as the S&P indexes.

VI. NASDAQ indexes—The NASDAQ Composite index includes all NASDAQ National Market System stocks plus all other NASDAQ domestic common stocks, totaling over 4,500 issues. The second largest NASDAQ index is the Industrial index, which contains over 3,000 stocks. Recent additions include the National Market Composite Index, the National Market Industrial Index, the NASDAQ 100 Index, and the Financial Index.

VII. Value Line indexes—The Value Line Geometric Average is composed of 1,700 stocks, about 80 percent of which are listed on the NYSE. The Value Line Arithmetic Average was introduced in 1988 and contains 1,700 stocks. For the Geometric Average, the daily price-relative average is calculated as a geometric mean of the stock price relative. A geometric mean is the nth root of n products. Thus the price relatives are multiplied together and the nth root taken. Both Value Line indexes are equally-weighted.

VIII. Other U.S. and foreign equity indexes.

A. The American Stock Exchange (AMEX) index is value-weighted and consists of all securities traded on the AMEX, including common shares, American depository receipts, and warrants. The AMEX index includes dividends paid as additions to the index.

B.   The Russell indexes—The Russell 3,000 consists of stocks of the 3,000 largest U.S. companies. The Russell 2,000 includes the 2,000 smaller-capitalization companies in the 3,000 index. The Russell 1000 is made up of the largest 1,000 companies. All the indexes are market-value weighted.

C.   Wilshire 5000 index—The Wilshire 5,000 includes all NYSE, AMEX and the larger OTC stocks—over 6,500 in all.

D.   Nikkei stock average—The Nikkei stock average includes 225 large firms on the Tokyo Stock Exchange. It is calculated like the Dow Jones Industrial Average using the divisor adjustment to compensate for stock splits and stock dividends.

E.   Tokyo Stock Price index (Topix)—Topix is a market-value-weighted index based on 1,055 companies listed on the first section of Tokyo Stock Exchange.

F.   Toronto Stock Exchange indexes—The Toronto Stock Exchange indexes consist of the Toronto Stock Exchange 300 and the Toronto Stock Exchange 35, which includes the 35 largest Canadian firms.

G.   Financial Times indexes—The Financial Times 30 index is a geometric average of 30 industrial stocks traded on the London Stock Exchange. The Financial Times 100 Share index (Footsie 100) is a market-value weighted index which consists of the 100 largest companies on the London Stock Exchange.

IX.   Bond market indicators.

A.   Shearson Lehman Hutton indexes include the Aggregate Index, the Government/ Corporate Bond Index, the Government Bond Index, the Corporate Bond Index, and the Treasury Bond Index. The Aggregate index consists of all publicly issued, non-convertible, domestic debt securities of the U.S. government and its agencies, and all publicly issued, non-convertible, domestic debt securities of the corporate classifications of industrial, utility, and financial. There are over 6,000 issues in the index.

B.   Merrill Lynch Bond indexes include the Corporate and Government Master index, the Corporate Master index, the Government Master index and the Domestic Master index.

C.   Salomon Brothers indexes consist of the Salomon Brothers High-Grade Bond index which includes corporate bonds rated AA or better with maturities of at least 12 years, and the Broad Investment-Grade Bond index.

X.   Indexes underlying options and futures contracts—A relatively new use for indexes is to serve as the underlying asset for options and futures contracts. The indexes are the Institutional Investor Index, the Major Market Index, the S&P 500 Index, the S&P 100 Index, the NYSE Composite Index, the Value Line stock average, and the Financial News Composite Index.

VOCABULARY REVIEW

systematic risk component
unsystematic risk component
market average
market index
blue-chip stock

geometric average
arithmetic average
matrix pricing
divisor adjustment procedure

SELF-TEST QUESTIONS

Definitional

1.   Factors affecting all securities in the market are called _____ components.

2.   _____ _____ are calculated by adding together the prices of the component stocks and dividing by the specified divisor.

3.   The 30 top-quality stocks in the Dow Jones Industrial Average are referred to as _____ _____ stocks.

4.   A _____ _____ is the nth root of n products.

5.   Unlike other market indicators, the _____ _____ _____ index includes dividends paid as additions to the index.

6.   A broad index which includes all the NYSE, AMEX, and the larger OTC stocks is the _____ _____ _____ index.

7.   The _____ stock average is the Japan's equivalent of the Dow Jones Industrial Average, and is designed to measure the performance of stocks on the Tokyo Stock Exchange.

8.   The most popular measures of security performance on the London Stock Exchange are the _____ _____ indexes.

9.   _____ _____ is a computer procedure to estimate the market price of a bond which does not trade on a particular day.

Conceptual

10.   The Dow Jones Industrial Average's divisor currently is less than one.

        a.   True   b.   False

11.   Factors unique to a particular firm, such as earning announcements and management
        changes, are called unsystematic risk components.

        a.   True   b.   False

12.   Market averages compare the current level of component securities' prices or market
        values with a base period value.

        a.   True   b.   False

13.   The 30 component stocks of the Dow Jones Industrial Average are never deleted because
        they are blue-chip stocks.

        a.   True   b.   False

14.   The Dow Jones Industrial Average is a price-weighted average.

        a.   True   b.   False

15.   The divisor of the Dow Jones Industrial Average is adjusted for stock splits and stock
        dividends, but not for changes in the component stocks.

        a.   True   b.   False

16.   The divisor adjustment procedure distorts the Dow Jones Industrial Average through time
        and creates a built-in bias for greater volatility in the average.

        a.   True   b.   False

17.   Because the Standard and Poor's 500 index is market-value-weighted, no adjustment for
        stock splits or stock dividends is necessary.

        a.   True   b.   False

18.   The NASDAQ Composite index is the broadest market indicator with over 6,000 issues.

        a.   True   b.   False

19. The Value Line Geometric Average becomes larger than the Arithmetic Average as time passes.

   a.   True   b.   False

20. Because the Value Line averages are equally-weighted, no adjustments for stock splits and stock dividends are necessary.

   a.   True   b.   False

21. The Wilshire 5000 Equity Index currently includes all NYSE, AMEX, and larger OTC stocks, totaling 5,000 in all.

   a.   True   b.   False

22. The Nikkei Stock Average is market-value-weighted, similar to the Standard and Poor's 500.

   a.   True   b.   False

23. The oldest and most popular bond index is the Shearson Lehman Hutton Government/ Corporate Bond Index.

   a.   True   b.   False

24. Salomon Brothers High-Grade Bond Index includes corporate bonds rated A or better with maturity of at least 12 years.

   a.   True   b.   False

25. Indexes can serve as the underlying asset for options and futures contracts which are used to hedge positions in stocks and bonds.

   a.   True   b.   False

26. Market indexes are used primarily as

   a.   a general indication of the market's performance.
   b.   a benchmark to measure the performance of investment managers.
   c.   an underlying asset for index futures and option contracts.
   d.   an indicator of future economic activity.
   e.   all of the above

27. Which of the following statements is most correct?

    a.   The Dow Jones Industrial Average is a good benchmark by which to measure the performance of investment managers.

    b.   The Dow Jones Industrial Average is the most popular market indicator with the business press in the United States.

    c.   The Dow Jones Industrial Average is market-value weighted.

    d.   The divisor adjustment procedure makes the Dow Jones Industrial Average less volatile through time.

    e.   All of the above statements are correct.

28. The Standard and Poor's 500 Composite Index has which of the following advantages?

    a.   It is an index number relative to a base period number. Thus its value is consistent and comparable through time.

    b.   Monthly values for the S&P 500 have been determined back to 1945.

    c.   The market value of the S&P 500 shares represents about 60 percent of the market value of all stocks listed on the NYSE.

    d.   The S&P 500 includes dividends paid as additions to the index.

    e.   All of the above statements are correct.

29. Which of the following statements is *most* correct?

    a.   All of the bond indexes use the matrix pricing technique.

    b.   The Shearson Lehman Hutton Aggregate Index has more than 6,000 issues.

    c.   The oldest and most popular bond index is the Shearson Lehman Hutton Government/Corporate Bond Index.

    d.   The Salomon Brothers high-grade bond index includes corporate bonds rated AA or better with maturities of at least 12 years.

    e.   All of the above statements are correct.

SELF-TEST PROBLEMS

(The following data apply to Self-Test Problems 1 through 9.)
Consider the following information about four securities:

Stock	Price		Shares Outstanding
	Thursday Close	Friday Close	
IBN	$ 60	$ 58	1,000
Eastman	100	110	500
Roebuck	40	45	80
Wendy	13	15	2,000

41

1. Assuming the divisor is 4, the price-weighted average for Thursday is

    a.   57.50.
    b.   55.13.
    c.   53.25.
    d.   54.25.
    e.   53.75.

2. The rate of return for the average from Thursday close to Friday close is

    a.   5.07 percent.
    b.   7.50 percent.
    c.   5.32 percent.
    d.   7.04 percent.
    e.   6.80 percent.

3. The market value of these four stocks on Thursday is

    a. $53,250.
    b. $139,200.
    c. $57,000.
    d. $130,200.
    e. $145,500.

4. Using the Thursday close market value as the denominator, the rate of return for the index from Thursday close to Friday close is

    a.   5.32 percent.
    b.   4.89 percent.
    c.   7.04 percent.
    d.   5.91 percent.
    e.   6.42 percent.

5. If you calculate the holding period return for each individual stock from Thursday to Friday close, then the arithmetic average return for the four stocks is

    a.   1.27 percent.
    b.   9.44 percent.
    c.   5.32 percent.
    d.   8.64 percent.
    e.   7.93 percent.

6.   If you invest an amount equal to the market value weight on Thursday for each stock, the rate of return on your portfolio for Friday is

  a.   8.24 percent.
  b.   5.97 percent.
  c.   5.34 percent.
  d.   6.44 percent.
  e.   none of the above

7.   Using the daily rates of return you calculated in Problem 5, the geometric average return for an equally-weighted portfolio of the four stocks is

  a.   8.40 percent.
  b.   5.34 percent.
  c.   8.64 percent.
  d.   7.40 percent.
  e.   none of the above

8.   Using the same procedure as used by Value Line and assuming the index is at 131.50 at Thursday close, the value of the average at Friday close is

  a.   138.52.
  b.   142.55.
  c.   140.32.
  d.   142.86.
  e.   144.55.

9.   Use the date for Thursday close. Assume that Eastman changes in price by 2 percent and the other stocks remain unchanged. The new value of the average is

  a.   55.00.
  b.   54.75.
  c.   57.00.
  d.   53.25.
  e.   none of the above

ANSWERS TO SELF-TEST QUESTIONS

1.	systematic risk	16.	True
2.	Market averages	17.	True
3.	blue-chip	18.	False
4.	geometric average	19.	False
5.	AMEX (American Stock Exchange)	20.	False
6.	Wilshire 5000 Equity	21.	False
7.	Nikkei	22.	False
8.	Financial Times	23.	True
9.	Matrix pricing	24.	False
10.	True	25.	True
11.	True	26.	e
12.	False	27.	b
13.	False	28.	a
14.	True	29.	e
15.	False		

SOLUTIONS TO SELF-TEST PROBLEMS

1.   c.   The price-weighted average for Thursday is:

$$\frac{\$60 + \$100 + \$40 + \$13}{4} = \$53.25$$

2.   d.   The price-weighted average for Friday is:

$$\frac{\$58 + \$110 + \$45 + \$15}{4} = \$57$$

The rate of return for the average from Thursday close to Friday close is:

$$\frac{\$57 - \$53.25}{\$53.25} = 7.04\%$$

3.   b.   The market value of these four stocks for Thursday is:
$\$60(1,000) + \$100(500) + \$40(80) + \$13(2,000) = \$139,200$

4.   a.   The market value of these four stocks for Friday is:
$58(1,000) + $110(500) + $45(80) + $15(2,000) = $146,600
The rate of return for the index from Thursday close to Friday close is:

$$\frac{\$146,600 - \$139,200}{\$139,200} = 5.32\%$$

5.   d.   The holding period return for each stock is:
IBN: ($58 − $60)/$60 = −3.33%
Eastman: ($110 − $100)/$100 = 10%
Roebuck: ($45 − $40)/$40 = 12.5%
Wendy: ($15 − $13)/$13 = 15.38%
The arithmetic return for these four stocks is:
(−3.33 + 10 + 12.5 + 15.38)/4 = 8.64%

6.   c.   The weight of each stock on Thursday is:
IBN: 60,000/139,200 = 43%
Eastman: 50,000/139,200 = 36%
Roebuck: 3,200/139,200 = 2%
Wendy: 26,000/139,200 = 19%
The rate of return on your portfolio for Friday is:
(−3.33)(43) + (10)(36) + (12.5)(2) + (15.38)(19) = 5.34%

7.   a.   The geometric average return for the four stocks is:
$[(0.967)(1.1)(1.125)(1.1538)]^{1/4} - 1 = 8.40\%$

8.   b.   The value of the average at Friday close is:
(1.084)(131.5) = 142.55

9.   e.   The new value of the average is:
(60 + 102 + 40 + 13)/4 = 53.75

CHAPTER 5

EFFICIENT CAPITAL MARKETS: A THEORY

OVERVIEW

This chapter provides an overview of the efficient market hypothesis and explains the following: (1) the weak-form, semistrong-form, and strong-form market efficiency; (2) the fair game, random-walk, submartingale, and martingale models; (3) the major empirical studies of market efficiency; and (4) the implications of the efficient market hypothesis to investors.

OUTLINE

I.   An efficient market is a market in which security prices correctly reflect all available information.

     A.   Weak-form efficiency—If markets are weak-form efficient, security prices reflect all past information.

     B.   Semistrong-form efficiency—Security prices reflect all publicly available information.

     C.   Strong-form efficiency—Security prices reflect all information that is known about a firm, even nonpublic information.

II.   In a perfectly efficient market, security prices fluctuate randomly around their true value and adjust instantaneously to new information. Furthermore, the price reactions are unbiased.

III. Theoretical models of security prices or returns.

     A.   The fair game model states that it is not possible to use all available information at time t to earn an abnormal return over the next period. Therefore, the expected

47

return on an asset will equal its actual return, or, stated differently, the expected deviation of the actual return from the expected return is zero:

$$E(\varepsilon_{i,t+1}) = r_{i,t+1} - E(r_{i,t+1}|\phi_t) = 0 \qquad (5.3)$$

B.   The martingale model describes a series of returns in which the best prediction about the next return is the last observed return. If returns conform to a martingale model, security prices will conform to a submartingale model. If the information set is the past sequence of stock prices, then the submartingale model is a test of weak-form efficiency described by the following equation:

$$E[P_{i,t+1}|P_{i,t}, P_{i,t-1}, ..., P_{i,t-n}] > P_{i,t} \qquad (5.5)$$

C.   The random-walk model states that successive changes in stock prices follow a random walk. Note that the change in stock price is also the stock's return, P_t/P_{t-1}, over a specified period. The random-walk model states that stock returns are identically distributed and independent.

$$f(r_{i,t+1}|r_{i,t}, r_{i,t-1}, ..., r_{i,t-n}) = f(r_{i,t}) \qquad (5.6)$$

where

$f(r_{i,t})$ = probability distribution of returns for security i for period $t - n$ to t.

IV.   Testing for market efficiency: any tests based on models of expected stock returns are joint tests of market efficiency and the model being used to describe expected returns.

A.   Tests using expected returns
   1.   Mean-adjusted returns.

$$AR_{i,t} = r_{i,t} - \bar{r}_i \qquad (5.7)$$

where $AR_{i,t}$ = abnormal return for security i in period t.

$\bar{r}_i$ = average return for security i oversome prior period.

   2.   Market-adjusted returns.
$AR_{i,t} = r_{i,t} - r_{M,t}$
where
$r_{M,t}$ = return a market index for period t.

3.   Market model returns.
$$r_{i,t} = \alpha_i + \beta_i r_{M,t} + \varepsilon_{i,t}$$
where

$\alpha_{i,t}$ = intercept term for security i

$\beta_{i,t}$ = slope of the regression line

$\varepsilon_{i,t}$ = error term

and $AR_{i,t} = r_{i,t} - (\alpha_i + \beta_i r_{M,t})$

V.   Tests of weak-form market efficiency.

A.   Tests of correlation in stock returns—If daily stock prices are positively correlated, an increase in stock price today will follow by an increase tomorrow. Thus, an implied strategy is to buy stocks when they begin to rise in price and sell when they begin to fall. However, the empirical evidence does not support this strategy because most correlations are small and not statistically significant.

B.   Tests of filter rules—A filter rule says to buy a stock if the price rises from a base price by the filter percentage, or more, and sell if it falls from a subsequent peak by the same filter percentage, at the same time selling short. The empirical evidence indicates that investors who must pay regular transaction costs have not been able to profit using a filter strategy.

C.   Tests of technical analysts' strategies—Several tests of standard trading rules used by technical analysts were performed and the results indicate that the weak-form market efficiency is not violated.

D.   Tests of market overreaction to information—The market overreaction hypothesis suggests that stocks that have fallen the most in price over the past two to three years will outperform stocks that have appreciated the most during the same period. Some studies found evidence that the market may overreact to new information, especially negative information about a firm.

E.   Occurrence of calendar-based patterns of stock returns.

1.   The January effect—The average return for stocks in January is much greater than the average for all other months, especially for small firms.
2.   Day-of-the-week effect—Returns on Monday are, on average, highly negative, whereas those on Wednesday and Friday are largely positive.

F.   Predicting returns using firm characteristics—Several studies find that small-capitalization firms and firms with low P/Es earn abnormal returns over extended periods. One study documents evidence of both P/E and firm-size effect. Smaller firms on average earn higher returns, but within each of the five firm-size categories, companies with lower P/Es have higher returns than those with higher P/Es.

G.   Predicting returns using financial variables—There is evidence that long-term stock returns (one to two years ahead) are related to certain financial variables such as the stock's dividend yield, earnings/price ratio, the level of interest rates, and business conditions.

VI.   Tests of semistrong-form market efficiency—Most empirical tests for semistrong-form efficiency take the form of an event study.

A.   Announcement of stock splits—Stocks that split begin rising in price about 30 months prior to the split and on average show no significant abnormal returns after the split. Results of this study are consistent with the efficient-market hypothesis.

B.   Dividend and earnings announcements—Information contained in earnings announcements is impounded into a security's price at the time of the announcement, except when the earnings are unexpectedly better or worse than the forecasted earnings. Some researchers report that abnormal returns can be earned by buying a security a few days prior to the dividend declaration date and selling it three days later.

C.   Recommendations by investment advisory services—Researchers who explore this topic report results generally consistent with semistrong-form efficiency.

D.   The Value Line service—When transaction costs are not included, strategies based on Value Line rankings outperform a buy-and-hold strategy. However, the inclusion of reasonable transaction costs removes most but not all of the excess profits.

VII.   Tests of strong-form market efficiency—If stock prices reflect all that is known by anyone at each point in time, the market is strong-form efficient. Few financial economists consider this extreme form of market efficiency to hold.

A.   Professional investment managers—Many studies document that, on average, a majority of mutual funds typically underperform broad indexes such as the S&P 500, based on risk-adjusted returns. In addition, their performance is not consistent from year to year.

B.   Stock exchange specialists—There is evidence that most specialist firms are highly profitable.

C.   Corporate insiders—A number of studies indicate that insiders do earn abnormal returns. The more informed insider, such as officer-directors or chairmen, predict future price behavior better than other insiders.

VIII.   Information and efficiency in the options and futures markets—Several studies indicate that options are priced relatively close to their theoretical values. Similar findings are reported for financial futures markets.

IX.   Implications of the efficient-market hypothesis for investors—The existence of securities markets that are at least semistrong-form efficient implies the following about investment management:

A.   Stock prices cannot be predicted.

B.   Analysis of individual securities in an attempt to find undervalued ones will not increase portfolio returns.

C.   Transaction costs should be minimized. Investors should adopt a buy-and-hold philosophy and trade as little as possible.

D.   Economies of scale should be exploited in portfolio management. It is more efficient to manage large sums of money than smaller amounts.

E.   The best portfolio management style is a passive one.

F.   There always will be winners and losers in the market. Just because some investors have outperformed the market over an extended period does not necessarily mean the market is not efficient.

G.   Investors should have a great degree of skepticism about investment advisors who claim that they consistently beat the market, and a great reluctance to pay for their services.

VOCABULARY REVIEW

efficient capital market
informational efficiency
weak-form efficiency
event study
derivative instruments
semistrong-form efficiency
strong-form efficiency
fair-game model
martingale model

submartingale model
random-walk model
mean-adjusted return
market-adjusted return
filter rule
market overreaction
january effect
day-of-the-week effect

SELF-TEST QUESTIONS

Definitional

1. _____ efficiency is the ability to provide trading services for consumers at the lowest possible transaction costs.

2. If security prices reflect all information contained in the past stock prices and trading volume, the market is _____ _____ efficient.

3. In an _____ market, security prices overreact or price reaction is not immediate.

4. If security returns conform to a martingale process, security prices will conform to a _____ _____ process.

5. The _____ _____ regresses the security's returns and the market's returns.

6. The market _____ hypothesis suggests that stocks that have fallen the most in price will outperform stocks that have risen the most in the same period.

7. The phenomenon that the average return for stocks in January is much greater than the average for all other months is referred to as the _____ _____.

8. The _____ _____ _____ hypothesis suggests that investors sell securities that have lost money in order to establish a capital loss for the year, thus reducing the taxable income.

9.	If stock prices reflect all information that is known by anyone at each point in time, the market is _____ _____ efficient.

10.	Securities whose values depend on the underlying asset are called _____ instruments.

Conceptual

11.	Allocational efficiency refers to the quick reaction of security prices to new information.

	a.	True				b.	False

12.	Prices of securities in markets that are semistrong-form efficient reflect all publicly available information about the companies.

	a.	True				b.	False

13.	Insider trading rules only cover trading by corporate insiders, not their relatives and associates.

	a.	True				b.	False

14.	In a perfectly efficient market, security prices sometimes can overreact to negative information.

	a.	True				b.	False

15.	The random-walk theory implies an irrational market because stock prices are determined randomly.

	a.	True				b.	False

16.	The random-walk model is more restrictive than the fair-game or martingale models.

	a.	True				b.	False

17.	The submartingale model says that the next period's security price will be greater than last period's price.

	a.	True				b.	False

18. The fair-game model places no restriction on the correlation of successive returns through time.

    a.   True   b.   False

19. Empirical tests based on equilibrium models are joint tests of market efficiency and the model being used to describe expected returns.

    a.   True   b.   False

20. The notion of weak-form market efficiency can be consistent with technical analysis.

    a.   True   b.   False

21. The strategy of buying stocks when they begin to rise and sell when they begin to fall is consistent with the weak-form market efficiency.

    a.   True   b.   False

22. The buy-and-hold strategy always outperforms the filter rule, even when you do not have to pay transaction costs.

    a.   True   b.   False

23. The existence of calendar-based patterns of stock returns is consistent with the weak-form market efficiency.

    a.   True   b.   False

24. The day-of-week effect documents that security returns on Mondays are, on average, negative whereas those on Wednesdays and Fridays are positive.

    a.   True   b.   False

25. Strategies based on P/E ratios call for investors to buy stocks with low P/Es and sell or avoid those with high P/Es.

    a.   True   b.   False

26 Most empirical tests for weak-form efficiency take the form of an event study.

    a.   True   b.   False

27. On average, a majority of mutual funds typically underperformed broad indexes, such as the S&P 500.

   a.   True   b.   False

28. If the market is strong-form efficient, even corporate insiders do not earn abnormal returns.

   a.   True   b.   False

29. Options or futures prices are useful predictors of future prices of their underlying asset at the time the contract expires.

   a.   True   b.   False

30. If the market is perfectly efficient, which of the following statements is *not* correct?

   a.   Prices will fluctuate randomly around their true value.
   b.   Price reaction will be unbiased.
   c.   Price reaction to new information will be instantaneous.
   d.   Security prices will overreact to negative information.
   e.   All of the above statements are correct.

31. Which of the following statements is *most* correct?

   a.   The random-walk model places no restriction on the correlation of successive returns through time.
   b.   The martingale model is more restrictive than the random-walk model.
   c.   The fair-game model is only concerned with the expected value of the security's return, whereas the random-walk model is based on the entire return distribution.
   d.   The martingale model requires successive returns to be independent.
   e.   All of the above statements are correct.

32. Which of the following is not a test of weak-form market efficiency?

   a.   Tests of correlation in stock returns
   b.   Tests of filter rules
   c.   Tests of technical analysts' strategies
   d.   Predicting returns using firm characteristics.
   e.   All of the above tests are tests of weak-form market efficiency.

33. Which one of the following tests in *not* a test of semistrong-form market efficiency?

    a.   Stock price reactions to the announcement of stock splits
    b.   Recommendations of the Value Line service
    c.   Profitability of stock exchange specialists
    d.   Recommendations by investment advisory services
    e.   Stock reactions to dividend and earnings announcements

34. Which of the following statements represents implications of the efficient market hypothesis for investors?

    a.   The best portfolio management style is a passive one.
    b.   Stock prices cannot be predicted.
    c.   Transaction costs should be minimized.
    d.   Economies of scale should be exploited in portfolio management.
    e.   All of the above statements are correct.

SELF-TEST PROBLEMS

Assume the following prices of Compaq Computer are:

Day	Stock Price
0	$25
1	26 *b*
2	28
3	31
4	30 S
5	28
6	30 *b*
7	31
8	30 S
9	28
10	27

1. If you follow the strategy of using a one percent filter rule, the days on which you would buy stock are

    a.   1,2,3,6, and 7.
    b.   2,3, and 7.
    c.   1, 6.
    d.   1,2,3, and 6.
    e.   1,5, and 6.

2. The days on which you would sell and short the stock are

 a. 4,8.
 b. 4,5,9, and 10.
 c. 4,8,9, and 10.
 d. 8,9, and 10.
 e. 4,8, and 10.

3. Ignoring transaction costs, the rate of return you earn by following the one percent filter rule is

 a. 12.80 percent.
 b. 25.00 percent.
 c. 31.23 percent.
 d. 6.20 percent.
 e. 23.50 percent.

4. The rate of return you earn from buying the stock on day 0 and selling it on day 10 is

 a. 4.00 percent.
 b. 5.50 percent.
 c. 6.25 percent.
 d. 8.00 percent.
 e. 9.50 percent.

5. The regression of Goodyear stock against the return for the Standard and Poor's 500 Index gives the following result:

$$r_{Goodyear} = 0.0021 + 1.05r_{S\&P}$$

real

If the market return is 0.13 or 13% and the Goodyear return is 0.16 or 16%, the abnormal return for Goodyear is

$Exp = 13.86$

 a. 13.86 percent.
 b. -2.14 percent. 2.14
 c. 2.14 percent.
 d. 0.86 percent.
 e. none of the above

(The following data apply to Self-Test Problems 6 through 8.)

Given the following prices for Union Carbide which announced its quarterly earnings on Thursday, Day 0.

Event Day	Day	Union Carbide	S&P 500
-2	Tuesday	18.00	445.0
-1	Wednesday	18.50	445.6
0	Thursday	19.25	444.1
+1	Friday	19.00	446.3
+2	Monday	18.75	445.8

6.   Using the ratio P_t / P_{t-1}, the rates of return for Union Carbide and the S&P 500 index on Thursday are

   a.   2.78 percent and 0.13 percent.
   b.   -1.30 percent and 4.95 percent.
   c.   4.05 percent and 0.34 percent.
   d.   4.05 percent and -0.34 percent.
   e.   none of the above

7.   The average daily returns for the previous six months were: Union Carbide = 1.0126 and the S&P 500 = 1.0081. Using the mean-adjusted return model, the abnormal return for Union Carbide on Wednesday is

   a.   0.0279.
   b.   0.0102.
   c.   0.0208.
   d.   0.0197.
   e.   none of the above

8.   Using the market-adjusted return model, the abnormal return for Monday for Union Carbide is

   a.   -0.0213.
   b.   0.0197.
   c.   0.0152.
   d.   -0.0214.
   e.   none of the above

ANSWERS TO SELF-TEST QUESTIONS

1.	Operational	18.	True
2.	weak-form	19.	True
3.	inefficient	20.	False
4.	submartingale	21.	False
5.	market model	22.	False
6.	overreaction	23.	False
7.	January effect	24.	True
8.	tax-loss selling	25.	True
9.	strong-form	26.	False
10.	derivative	27.	True
11.	False	28.	True
12.	True	29.	False
13.	False	30.	d
14.	False	31.	c
15.	False	32.	d
16.	True	33.	c
17.	True	34.	e

SOLUTIONS TO SELF-TEST PROBLEMS

1. c. You buy on days 1 and 6 because the stock increases by at least one percent from the previous low price. Note that you do not buy additional shares if you already have a long position.

2. a. You sell and short the stock on days 4 and 8 because the stock declines by at least one percent from the previous high price.

3. b. The rate of return for long positions is:
    15% (day 1 to day 4) + 0% (day 6 to day 8) = 15%
    The rate of return for short positions is:
    0% (day 4 to day 6) + 10% (day 8 to day 10) = 10%
    The rate of return you earn by following the one percent filter rule is:
    15% + 10% = 25%

4. d. The rate of return you earn from buying the stock from day 0 and selling it on day 10 is:
    ($27 − $25)/$25 = 8%

5. c. The abnormal return for Goodyear is:
    16% − [0.21 + (1.05)(13%)] = 2.14%

6.   d.   The rate of return for Union Carbide on Thursday is:
          $(19.25/18.50) - 1 = 4.05\%$
          The rate of return for the S&P 500 on Thursday is:
          $(441.1/445.6) - 1 = -0.34\%$

7.   e.   Using the mean-adjusted return model, the abnormal return for Union Carbide on Wednesday is:
          $(18.50/18) - 1.0126 = 0.0152$

8.   a.   Using the market-adjusted return model, the abnormal return for Union Carbide on Monday is:
          $(18.75/19) - 1.0081 = -0.0213$

CHAPTER 6

MEASURING EXPECTED RETURN AND RISK FOR INDIVIDUAL SECURITIES AND PORTFOLIOS

OVERVIEW

This chapter describes how to measure risk and expected return for securities and portfolio, and explains the following: (1) the concept of diversification and why diversification reduces risk, (2) the efficient frontier, and (3) historical patterns of risk and return for domestic and international securities.

OUTLINE

I. Steps in the management of investment portfolios—A brief review. The quantitative portfolio management can be divided into four steps: security analysis, portfolio analysis, portfolio selection, performance evaluation, and revision.

II. Measuring the rate of return for financial securities.

   The rate of return on a security or the holding period yield (HPY) is calculated as:

   $$HPY_{i,t} = \frac{P_{i,t} + CF_{i,t} - P_{i,t-1}}{P_{i,t-1}} \qquad (6.1)$$

   where

   $HPY_{i,t}$ = the holding period yield on security i for time period t.
   $P_{i,t-1}$ = the price of security i at the beginning of period t.
   $P_{i,t}$ = the price of security i at the end of period t.
   $CF_{i,t}$ = the cash flow received on security i during time period t.

III. Random variables, probability distributions and evaluating the return, and risk of individual securities.

   A. A random variable is a measure whose outcome is unknown but can be characterized and analyzed through its probability distribution.

61

B.   The subjective method of producing a probability distribution of returns is an approach wherein the investor assesses the possible economic conditions for the foreseeable future, assigns probabilities to these various scenarios, and then determines what return the security will have under each scenario.

C.   An alternative approach for the construction of probability distributions of returns is to use actual historical returns for the security as a proxy for the return distribution. This method assigns equal probabilities to historical returns.

IV.   Using the historical method requires adjusting for stock splits and stock dividends.

V.   Evaluating the return distribution.

A.   Measuring the average return—There are four common measures to evaluate the average return.

      1.   The mode is the return that has the highest probability of occurring.
      2.   The median is the middle value of the return distribution.
      3.   The expected return or the arithmetic mean is a weighted average of all possible returns, where the weights are the probabilities assigned to each return.

$$\textit{Arithmetic mean} = E(r_1) = \sum_{t=1}^{T} r_t / T \qquad (6.2)$$

where $E(r_i)$ is the expected return, and the weights are all equal to $1/T$.

      4.   The geometric mean is a weighted average of possible returns where the returns are multiplied rather than added. When using historical returns, the geometric mean is calculated as:

$$\textit{Geometric mean} = G$$
$$= [(1+r_1)(1+r_2)(1+r_3)...(1+r_T)]^{\frac{1}{T}} - 1 \qquad (6.3)$$

B.   Measuring the risk—There are four popular measures of risk.

      1.   The mean absolute deviation is the average of the absolute value of each deviation.

2.   The variance is the average of the squared deviations about the mean. When using a sample of historical returns, the variance is computed as:

$$Variance = \sigma^2 = \sum_{t=1}^{T} (r_t - E(r_t))^2/(T-1) \tag{6.7}$$

The square root of the variance, the standard deviation, is more commonly used because it measures risk in the same units as the mean. The standard deviation is:

$$Standard\ deviation = \sigma = \sqrt{\sigma^2} \tag{6.8}$$

3.   The semivariance measures only return deviations below the mean.
4.   For securities whose return distributions are not normal, a risk measure called skewness is used. Skewness is the average of the cubed deviations from the mean. Relative skewness is the third moment scaled by the standard deviation cubed, (m^3/σ^3).

VI.   Measuring the expected return and risk for a portfolio.

A.   A portfolio's return is a weighted average of the component securities' returns. The weights are the proportionate amount of total investment dollars placed in each security.

B.   Measuring the risk in a portfolio.

1.   Covariance between security returns—The covariance measures the degree of association between two returns.
2.   Correlation also measures the degree of association between two returns, but the magnitude of the correlation is not affected by the units of measurements of the variables. Consequently, it will always be between -1 and +1.
3.   Variance of a portfolio: the general formula for the variance of a portfolio of a securities is:
$$\sigma_n^2 = E[r_n - E(r_n)]^2$$

$$\sigma_n^2 = \sum_{i=1}^{n} W_i^2 \sigma_i^2 + \sum_{i=1}^{n}\sum_{j=1}^{n} W_i W_j \sigma_{ij}, \ i \neq j \tag{6.17}$$

VII.   Effects of correlation—How correlation can affect the risk of a portfolio. When the returns on the two securities are perfectly positively correlated, the standard deviation of the portfolio is a weighted average of the standard deviations of the individual securities. If the two securities rates of return are perfectly negatively correlated, the portfolio's standard deviation is the difference between the weighted average of the two standard deviations. In general, the portfolio's standard deviation falls as the correlation coefficient declines.

VIII.   The mapping of the set of portfolios that maximize expected return for each and every level of risk is called the efficient set or efficient frontier.

IX.   The benefits from extended diversification—As portfolio size increases, risk will fall and continue falling until all possible securities are included in the portfolio. Investors who hold both domestic and foreign securities get greater diversification benefits than investors who invest in only domestic securities.

VOCABULARY REVIEW

holding period yield	variance
random variable	semivariance
probability distribution	skewness
median	covariance
mode	correlation coefficient
arithmetic mean	efficient frontier
geometric mean	international diversification
mean absolute deviation	nonsystematic risk

SELF-TEST QUESTIONS

Definitional

1.   A _____ _____ is a measure whose outcome is unknown but can be characterized through its probability distribution.

2.   The return that has the highest probability of occurring is called the _____.

3.   If all the returns are ranked from smallest to largest, the return in the middle is the _____.

4.   The expected return which is the weighted average of all possible returns is called the _____ _____.

5.   The _____ of an investment is the uncertainty concerning the expected return.

6.   The square root of the variance is the _____ _____.

7.   The _____ measures return deviations below the mean.

8.   When stock returns are normally distributed, the _____ completely describes the dispersion characteristics of the distribution.

9.   _____ is a risk measure that evaluates unusually large or small returns in the return distribution.

10.   The statistical value that measures the degree of association between two variables is called the _____.

11.   The _____ _____ is the mapping of the set of portfolios that maximizes expected return for each and every level of risk.

Conceptual

12.   Portfolio analysis deals with developing and analyzing the probability return distributions for securities that the investor is considering purchasing.

      a.   True   b.   False

13.   The holding period yield is the annualized rate of return of a financial security.

      a.   True   b.   False

14.   When constructing a probability return distribution, the sum of all probabilities must equal one and each probability must be nonnegative.

      a.   True   b.   False

15.   The first step of the objective method of producing a probability distribution of returns is the determination of probabilities for the various economic scenarios.

      a.   True   b.   False

16.   When analyzing historical return distributions, price and cash dividend data must be adjusted for any stock splits or stock dividends.

      a.   True   b.   False

17.   A summary measure is a statistic that represents a particular feature of the return distribution.

      a.   True   b.   False

18.	The median is the return that has the highest probability of occurring.

	a.	True		b.	False

19.	The geometric mean is appropriate if you are concerned with the average expected return over several successive periods.

	a.	True		b.	False

20.	The expected return or arithmetic mean is more commonly used than the geometric mean.

	a.	True		b.	False

21.	The mean absolute deviation is the most popular measure of risk.

	a.	True		b.	False

22.	For a normal distribution, the semivariance adds no additional information about the risk of a security to that contained in the variance.

	a.	True		b.	False

23.	Investors should diversify because diversification can reduce portfolio risk while leaving expected return the same.

	a.	True		b.	False

24.	A portfolio's risk is a weighted average of the component securities' risks.

	a.	True		b.	False

25.	A positive covariance means that the two securities' returns tend to move in the same direction.

	a.	True		b.	False

26.	The correlation measures the degree of association between two securities' returns but the magnitude of the correlation is not affected by the units of measurement of the variables.

	a.	True		b.	False

27.	By diversifying internationally, investors can achieve lower levels of systematic risk than are possible through domestic diversification.

	a.	True		b.	False

28. The common measure(s) to evaluate the average value is/are

   a.   the mode.
   b.   the median.
   c.   the arithmetic mean.
   d.   the geometric mean.
   e.   all of the above

29. Which of the following statements is *incorrect*?

   a.   The risk of the investment is the uncertainty concerning the expected return.
   b.   The semivariance measures return deviations below the mean.
   c.   The variance is the square root of the standard deviation.
   d.   The mean absolute deviation computes the average of the absolute value of each deviation.
   e.   All of the above statements are correct.

30. Which of the following statements is *most* correct?

   a.   The variance is a statistical value that measures the degree of association between two variables.
   b.   The correlation coefficient is always between -1 and +1.
   c.   As the number of securities in the portfolio increases, both systematic and nonsystematic risks will decline.
   d.   When the correlation coefficient is zero, the risk of a two-security portfolio is a weighted average of the component securities' risk.
   e.   All of the above statements are correct.

SELF-TEST PROBLEMS

A stock that pays no dividend is currently selling at $50. The possible prices for which the stock might sell at the end of one year, with associated probabilities are:

Stock Price	Probability
$40	0.1
$45	0.2
$50	0.4
$58	0.2
$66	0.1

1. The expected return of the stock at the end of the year is:

   a. 10.4 percent.
   b. 2.4 percent.
   c. 9.5 percent.
   d. 4.2 percent.
   e. none of the above

2. The standard deviation of the expected return is

   a. 20.8 percent.
   b. 10.4 percent.
   c. 14.4 percent.
   d. 9.5 percent.
   e. none of the above

(The following data apply to Self-Test Problems 3 through 6.)

Consider the following expected return, variance, and correlation coefficients for three securities listed below:

Security	Expected Return	Variance	Cor(1,2)	Cor(1,3)	Cor(2,3)
1	10%	16	.70	-.20	.50
2	14%	25			
3	9%	9			

3. If you put 50 percent of your money in stock 1 and 50 percent in stock 2, the expected return of the portfolio is

   a. 11 percent.
   b. 11.5 percent.
   c. 13 percent.
   d. 12 percent.
   e. none of the above

4. The standard deviation of the portfolio in Problem 3 is

   a. 4.2 percent.
   b. 5.9 percent.
   c. 17.3 percent.
   d. 7.5 percent.
   e. none of the above

5. The expected return of an equally weighted portfolio of the three stocks is

   a. 11.5 percent.
   b. 13 percent.
   c. 11 percent.
   d. 10.5 percent.
   e. none of the above

6. The standard deviation of an equally weighted portfolio of the three stocks is

   a. 9.6 percent.
   b. 5.2 percent.
   c. 4.5 percent.
   d. 3.1 percent.
   e. none of the above

(The following data apply to Self-Test Problems 7 and 8.)

Consider the following expected return and standard deviation values for the two securities listed below:

Security	E(r)	σ
AAR	6%	5%
CBS	11%	9%

7. When $W_{AAR} = W_{CBS} = 0.50$, and $W_{AAR} = 0.25$ and $W_{CBS} = 0.75$, the portfolio expected returns are, respectively

   a. 8.50 percent and 7.25 percent.
   b. 7.00 percent and 9.75 percent.
   c. 6.00 percent and 11.00 percent
   d. 8.00 percent and 8.75 percent.
   e. 8.50 percent and 9.75 percent.

8. Assume that $W_{AAR} = W_{CBS}$. When the correlation coefficient values are -1, 0, and +1, the portfolio standard deviations are, respectively

   a. 2.00 percent, 5.15 percent, and 7.00 percent.
   b. 2.00 percent, 7.00 percent, and 9.00 percent.
   c. 3.91 percent, 5.15 percent, and 7.00 percent.
   d. 5.00 percent, 7.10 percent, and 9.00 percent.
   e. none of the above

ANSWERS TO SELF-TEST QUESTIONS

1.	random variable	16.	True
2.	mode	17.	True
3.	median	18.	False
4.	arithmetic mean	19.	True
5.	risk	20.	True
6.	standard deviation	21.	False
7.	semivariance	22.	True
8.	variance	23.	True
9.	Skewness	24.	False
10.	covariance	25.	True
11.	efficient frontier	26.	True
12.	False	27.	True
13.	False	28.	e
14.	True	29.	c
15.	False	30.	b

SOLUTIONS TO SELF-TEST PROBLEMS

1. b. The rate of return of the stock corresponding to the year-end stock price of $40 is:

$$(\$40-\$50)/\$50 = -20\%$$

The remaining rates of returns are: -10%, 0%, 16%, 32%

The expected return of the stock is:

$$(-20)(0.1) + (-10)(0.2) + (0)(0.4) + (16)(0.2) + (32)(0.1) = 2.4\%$$

2. c. The standard deviation of the stock is:

$$[(-20-2.4)^2(.1) + (-10-2.4)^2(.2) + (0-2.4)^2(.4)$$
$$+ (16-2.4)^2(.2) + (32-2.4)^2(.1)]^{1/2}$$
$$= (207.84)^{1/2} = 14.42\%$$

3. d. The expected return of the portfolio is:

$$E(r) = (10\%)(.5) + (14\%)(.5) = 12\%$$

4. a. The variance of the portfolio is:

$$(.5)^2(16) + (.5)^2(25) + 2(.5)(.5)(.7)(4)(5)$$
$$= 4 + 6.25 + 7 = 17.25$$

The standard deviation of the portfolio is:

$$(17.25)^{1/2} = 4.15\%$$

5. c. The expected return of an equally-weighted of portfolio of three stocks is:

$$E(r) = (10 + 14 + 9)/3 = 11\%$$

6. d. The variance of the portfolio is:
$(.33)^2(16) + (.33)^2(25) + (.33)^2(9) + 2(.33)(.33)(.7)(4)(5) + 2(.33)(.33)(-.2)(4)(3)$
$+ 2(.33)(.33)(.5)(5)(3)$
$= 1.74 + 2.72 + 0.98 + 3.05 - 0.52 + 1.63 = 9.6$
The standard deviation of the portfolio is:
$(9.6)^{1/2} = 3.10\%$

7. e. When $W_{AAR} = W_{CBS} = 0.5$, the portfolio expected return is:
$(6\%)(0.5) + (11\%)(0.5) = 8.5\%$
When $W_{AAR} = 0.25$ and $W_{CBS} = 0.75$, the portfolio expected return is:
$(6\%)(0.25) + (11\%)(0.75) = 9.75\%$

8. a. When the correlation coefficient is -1, the portfolio standard deviation is:
$[(0.5)^2(5)^2 + (0.5)^2(9)^2 + 2(0.5)(0.5)(-1)(5)(9)]^{1/2} = 2\%$
When the correlation coeficient is 0, the portfolio standard deviation is:
$[(0.5)^2(5)^2 + (0.5)^2(9)^2]^{1/2} = 5.15\%$
When the correlation coeficient is +1, the portfolio standard deviation is:
$[(0.5)^2(5)^2 + (0.5)^2(9)^2 + 2(0.5)(0.5)(5)(9)]^{1/2} = 7\%$

CHAPTER 7

FINDING THE EFFICIENT FRONTIER

OVERVIEW

This chapter shows you the data needed to identify the efficient set of portfolios and illustrates the following: (1) the graphical relationship between expected return and risk and how these two variables interact to identify the efficient set, (2) how to derive the efficient frontier graphically using the Markowitz mean-variance-covariance model, (3) how to derive the efficient set mathematically, and (4) how to determine how restrictions on short selling can alter the efficient frontier.

OUTLINE

I. Formalizing the investor's objective—Risk-averse investors should strive to minimize risk at their desired level of expected return. To solve for the set of risk-minimizing portfolios, we need estimates of expected return, variance, and covariance.

II. Graphical analysis of the efficient frontier—The graphical approach to solving for the efficient frontier for a sample of three securities can be summarized in five steps: (1) convert formulas for portfolio expected return and variance into expressions containing any two of the securities' weights; (2) graph the isomean, or equal expected-return, lines; (3) find the minimum-variance portfolio; (4) graph the isovariance or equal-variance ellipses; and (5) identify the critical line, or the efficient set.

III. A mathematical derivation of the efficient frontier.

$$\textit{Minimize: } \sigma_n^2 = \sum_{i=1}^{n} W_i^2 \sigma_i^2 + \sum_{i=1}^{n}\sum_{j=1}^{n} W_i W_j \sigma_{ij} \quad , i \neq j \tag{7.1}$$

subject to:

$$\sum_{i=1}^{n} W_i E(r_i) = E^* \tag{7.2}$$

$$\sum_{i=1}^{n} W_i = 1 \tag{7.3}$$

73

Where E^* is the desired level of the expected return. This problem can be solved using calculus and the technique of Lagrange multipliers.

IV. Efficient set analysis with no short selling—Because short-selling restrictions place additional constraints on the optimization problem, the efficient frontier under these conditions will, in general, be lower than the frontier with no restrictions.

V. Selection of an optimal portfolio—The role of expected utility. As long as investors select portfolios along the efficient frontier, they will not only be maximizing their expected utility, but they will also be choosing the portfolio that minimizes risk at their desired expected return. The expected utility is maximized where the indifference curve set is tangent to the efficient frontier. Thus, the optimal portfolio that is best for you is that efficient portfolio that lies at the tangency point between your utility indifference curves and the efficient frontier. Because individuals have different risk and expected-return preferences, each investor will probably choose a different efficient portfolio.

VOCABULARY REVIEW

efficient frontier	critical line
quadratic programming	indifference curves
inequality constraints	expected utility
isomean lines	point of tangency
isovariance ellipses	minimum variance portfolio

SELF-TEST QUESTIONS

Definitional

1. The _____ lines are equal expected return lines.

2. Portfolios that have the same variance lie on an _____ _____.

3. The line that connects all the efficient portfolios is called the _____ _____.

4. _____ portfolios are portfolios whose risk/expected return profiles are dominated.

5. An investor's expected utility towards risk and expected return is represented graphically by a set of _____ curves.

Conceptual

6. The graphical approach can be used to identify the efficient set for portfolios containing no more than two securities.

    a. True   b. False

7. A negative weight of a security implies that the security must be sold short.

    a. True   b. False

8. To solve for the set of risk-minimizing portfolios, you only need to estimate the expected returns and variances of all the securities.

    a. True   b. False

9. The term isomean line means that all portfolios lying along the same line have the same expected return.

    a. True   b. False

10. All the portfolios on the critical line are efficient.

    a. True   b. False

11. The efficient frontier with no short selling is identical to the efficient frontier with no restrictions.

    a. True   b. False

12. All the combinations of expected return and risk on an indifference curve have the same expected utility for an investor.

    a. True   b. False

13. Three commonly used approaches to minimize risk at a given level of expected return are

    a.   graphical procedure.
    b.   calculus.
    c.   quadratic programming.
    d.   all of the above
    e.   none of the above

14. The variables necessary to solve for the set of risk-minimizing portfolios are

    a.   expected return.
    b.   variance.
    c.   covariance.
    d.   all of the above
    e.   Only variables a and b are necessary.

15. Which of the following statements is *most* correct?

    a.   The graphical approach can be used to identify the efficient set for portfolios containing no more than four securities.
    b.   All portfolios on the isovariance ellipse have the same variance.
    c.   To solve for the set of risk-minimizing portfolios, short selling is never allowed.
    d.   Calculus can be used to derive the efficient frontier for portfolios containing no more than 20 stocks.
    e.   None of the above statements are correct.

SELF-TEST PROBLEMS

1. Which one of the following portfolios cannot lie on the efficient frontier?

Portfolio	Expected Return	Standard Deviation
A	6%	11%
B	11%	19%
C	10%	25%
D	16%	33%

    a.   portfolio A
    b.   portfolio C
    c.   portfolios A and C
    d.   portfolios B and C
    e.   none of the above

(The following data apply to Self-Test Problems 2 through 4.)

You are given the following information on stocks of IBM and GE.

Stock	Expected Return	Standard Deviation
IBM	9%	20%
GE	10%	25%

2.   Assume that IBM and GE are uncorrelated. Find the percentage invested in IBM that will lead to the minimum variance portfolio.

    a.   61%
    b.   50%
    c.   65%
    d.   39%
    e.   none of the above

3.   What is the expected return of the minimum variance portfolio found in Problem 2?

    a.   9.61%
    b.   9.50%
    c.   10.00%
    d.   9.39%
    e.   none of the above

4.   What is the standard deviation of the minimum variance portfolio found in Problem 2?

    a.   22.50%
    b.   18.34%
    c.   15.62%
    d.   21.95%
    e.   none of the above

5.   The expected returns for AT&T (#1), GTE (#2), and MCI (#3) are 8 percent, 11 percent, and 13 percent, respectively. Which of the portfolio combinations listed below satisfies the desired expected return of 10 percent?

    a. $W_1 = 0.3$, $W_2 = 0.7$, $W_3 = 0.0$
    b. $W_1 = 0.4$, $W_2 = 0.5$, $W_3 = 0.1$
    c. $W_1 = 0.5$, $W_2 = 0.3$, $W_3 = 0.2$
    d. $W_1 = 0.6$, $W_2 = 0.1$, $W_3 = 0.3$
    e.   All of the above portfolio combinations satisfy the desired expected return of 10 percent.

ANSWERS TO SELF-TEST QUESTIONS

1.	isomean		9.	True
2.	isovariance ellipse		10.	True
3.	critical line		11.	False
4.	Inefficient		12.	True
5.	indifference		13.	d
6.	False		14.	d
7.	True		15.	b
8.	False			

SOLUTIONS TO SELF-TEST PROBLEMS

1.   b.   Portfolio C cannot lie on the efficient frontier because it has lower expected return and larger standard deviation than portfolio B.

2.   a.   The weight of IBM that will lead to the minimum variance portfolio can be found using calculus or by the following formulas:

$$w_{IBM} = \frac{\sigma_2^2 - \sigma_1\sigma_2 r_{12}}{\sigma_1^2 + \sigma_2^2 - 2\sigma_1\sigma_2 r_{12}}$$

$$w_{IBM} = \frac{(25)^2 - (20)(25)(0)}{(20)^2 + (25)^2 - 2(20)(25)(0)} = 61\%$$

3.   d.   The expected return of the minimum variance portfolio is:
$$E(r_p) = (9\%)(0.61) + (10\%)(0.39) = 9.39\%$$

4.   c.   The standard deviation of the minimum variance portfolio is:
$$\sigma(r_p) = [(0.61)^2(20)^2 + (0.39)^2(25)^2]^{1/2} = 15.62\%$$

5.   b.   For $E^* = 0.10$, consider the formula for portfolio expected return:
$$E(r) = W_1 E(r_1) + W_2 E(r_2) + (1-W_1-W_2)E(r_3)$$
Inserting the values for $E(r_1)$, $E(r_2)$, $E(r_3)$ and 0.10 for $E(r)$:
$$0.10 = 0.13 - (0.05)W_1 - (0.02)W_2$$
The only portfolio combination which satisfies the above equation is:
$$W_1 = 0.4, \; W_2 = 0.5, \; W_3 = 0.1$$

CHAPTER 8

THE SINGLE-INDEX MODEL

OVERVIEW

This chapter describes the single-index model and illustrates the following: (1) how the single-index model is developed and how the beta for a security is estimated, (2) how to use the single-index model as a method for generating the inputs required to derive the efficient frontier, (3) how the model can be used to decompose a security's total risk into the unsystematic and systematic risk components, and (4) how to recognize some of the problems associated with the estimation of beta and the use of the single-index model.

OUTLINE

I. Description and estimation of the single-index model—The return on any security or portfolio is a linear function of the return on a market index.

$$r_{i,t} = \alpha_i + \beta_i r_{M,t} + \epsilon_{i,t} \qquad (8.1)$$

where

$r_{i,t}$ = return on security i at time t

$r_{M,t}$ = return on the market index at time t

α_i = constant term

β_i = sensitivity of the security's return to changes in the market's return.

$\varepsilon_{i,t}$ = error term

A. Estimation of the model—The single-index, or market, model formulation of a security's return is usually estimated through regression. The regression technique most often used is the method of ordinary least squares (OLS). The OLS method finds the estimated values for α_i and β_i that minimize the sum of the squared errors.

By doing so, the estimated model that provides the best fit to the data can be approximated. The values for α_i and β_i that minimize the sum of the squared errors are:

$$\beta_i = \sigma_{i,M}/\sigma_M^2 \tag{8.3}$$

$$\alpha_i = E(r_i) - \beta_i E(r_M) \tag{8.4}$$

B. An illustration—An illustration of how the parameters of the single-index model can be estimated is provided in the text for McDonald's, TECO, and Wal-Mart.

C. Evaluation of the regression results—While the values of α_i and β_i give an indication of the direction of the relationship, in general, the magnitudes of these two coefficients do not necessarily measure how strong the relationship is between the security and the market index. The objective of the regression model is to explain as much as possible of the total variance of a security return. The total variance of a security can be decomposed into two elements:

$$\sigma_i^2 = \beta_i^2 \sigma_M^2 + \sigma_{\epsilon,i}^2 \tag{8.5}$$

the first element of total variance, $\beta_i^2 \sigma_M^2$, is the market-related portion of variance, whereas the $\sigma_{\epsilon i}^2$ is the firm-specific portion of total risk.

II. The single-index model and the efficient frontier—The single-index model developed by Sharpe can be used to provide a close approximation to the Markowitz model's efficient frontier at a fraction of the time and cost.

A. Assumptions and Input requirements.

1. Assumptions—The single-index model reduces the number of input computations by assuming that all pairwise covariances between individual securities are zero. To allow for interrelations among securities, the model assumes that these covariance effects can be captured by relating all securities' returns to a market index.

2. Input requirements—The model requires $3n + 2$ inputs for a sample of n securities: n estimates of α_i, n estimates of β_i, n estimates of the variance of ϵ_i, one estimate of $E(r_M)$, and one estimate of the variance of the market index.

B. Formulation of portfolio expected return and variance: using the assumptions underlying the single index model, the expected return and variance for a portfolio are:

$$E(r_n) = \sum_{i=1}^{n+1} W_i \alpha_i \qquad (8.13)$$

$$\sigma^2 = \sum_{i=1}^{n+1} W_i^2 \sigma_{\epsilon,i}^2 \qquad (8.14)$$

C. Formulation of the investor's objective—In deriving the efficient frontier using the single-index model, the investor seeks to solve the following problem:

$$\textit{Minimize:}\ \ \sigma_n^2 = \sum_{i=1}^{n+1} W_i^2 \sigma_{\epsilon,i}^2 \qquad (8.15)$$

$$\textit{Subject to:}\ \ \sum_{i=1}^{n+1} W_i \alpha_i = E^* \qquad (8.16)$$

$$\sum_{i=1}^{n} W_i = 1 \qquad (8.17)$$

$$\sum_{i=1}^{n} W_i\, \beta_i = W_{n+1} \qquad (8.18)$$

Where E^* is the desired level of the expected return. The single-index model seeks to minimize risk for each and every level of desired return, E^*, with the sum of all investment proportions summing to 1. The portfolio beta, $\Sigma W_i \beta_i$ is equal to the weight on the market index, W_{n+1}.

D. Derivation of the efficient frontier—A derivation of the efficient frontier for portfolios containing McDonald's, TECO, and Wal-Mart is provided in the text.

E.	Comparison of the Markowitz and Sharpe efficient frontiers—Because the Markowitz model takes into account the full covariance structure of returns, the Markowitz efficient frontier is higher than the Sharpe efficient set. However, the Sharpe model frontier is very close and does not require the calculation of many pairwise covariances.

III.	Diversification, risk decomposition, and the single-index model. A portfolio's risk contains two elements: the average value of the error variance of the securities in the portfolio and the portfolio's market risk. As the number of securities in the portfolio increases, the error variance portion becomes negligible.

IV.	Special problems with the single-index model.

A.	Invalid assumptions of the model—The Sharpe single-index model assumes that there is no correlation between security errors and that there is no correlation between the unique risk of a security and its market risk. Several empirical studies have documented that these assumptions are violated. However, the violation is probably not very serious.

B.	Beta estimation—Many studies have documented that portfolio betas are much more stable than betas of individual securities. Moreover, regression estimates of beta tend to regress toward their mean value of 1 over time. Therefore, investors must adjust beta estimates for this effect in order to obtain more reliable estimates.

VOCABULARY REVIEW

single-index model   error term
market risk   efficient frontier
firm-specific risk   stationary beta
ordinary least squares   regression tendency
ρ^2 error covariance

SELF-TEST QUESTIONS

Definitional

1.	In the single-index model equation, the _____ _____ represents the portion of the security's return that is not captured by α_i and β_i.

2.	The sensitivity of the security's return to changes in the market's return is called _____.

3.	The _____ _____ _____ method finds the values of the regression coefficients that minimize the sum of the squared errors.

4.	The _____ risk is the unique or firm-specific portion of total risk.

Conceptual

5.	The single-index model assumes that the return on any security is a linear or curvilinear function of the market return.

	a.	True			b.	False

6.	The single-index model was developed by Harry Markowitz.

	a.	True			b.	False

7.	The constant term in the single-index model measures the portion of the security's expected return that is not related to the market return.

	a.	True			b.	False

8.	The error term in the single-index model equation is expected to be zero.

	a.	True			b.	False

9.	The single-index model assumes that the variance of the error terms is constant for all securities.

	a.	True			b.	False

10.	The single-index model allows serial correlation among the error terms.

	a.	True			b.	False

11.	Whenever the security beta is less than 1, the security return will be more volatile than the market return.

	a.	True			b.	False

12.	The single-index model formulation of a security's return is usually estimated through regression.

	a.	True			b.	False

13. The objective of the regression model is to explain as much as possible of the total variance of a security's return.

   a.   True   b.   False

14. The single-index model assumes that all pairwise covariances between individual securities are zero.

   a.   True   b.   False

15. The single-index model requires more input computations than the Markowitz model.

   a.   True   b.   False

16. The single-index model assumes that security correlations can be sufficiently accounted for through the market index.

   a.   True   b.   False

17. The single-index model and the Markowitz model derive an identical efficient frontier.

   a.   True   b.   False

18. The gain through the reduction in portfolio variance from diversification becomes larger as the size of the portfolio is increased.

   a.   True   b.   False

19. Because the assumptions of the single-index model are usually violated, the derived efficient frontier is not valid.

   a.   True   b.   False

20. Ordinary least squares regression estimates of beta tend to move toward the mean value of one.

   a.   True   b.   False

21.   Which of the following is *not* an assumption of the single-index model?

    a.   There is no correlation among the error terms across securities.
    b.   Each security's error terms are uncorrelated with the returns of the market.
    c.   The variance about the error is constant for all securities.
    d.   The average error term is always equal to one.
    e.   All of the above statements are assumptions of the single-index model.

22.   Which of the following statements is *most* correct?

    a.   The single-index model's derived efficient frontier usually dominates the Markowitz efficient frontier.
    b.   Because the single-index model requires fewer computations, it can achieve similar results as the Markowitz model at a fraction of the cost.
    c.   The single-index model uses pairwise covariances of securities in its regression.
    d.   Individual security betas are more stable than portfolio betas.
    e.   All of the above statements are correct.

SELF-TEST PROBLEMS

(The following data apply to Self-Test Problems 1 through 3.)

In using the single-index model, a Merrill Lynch security analyst estimates the relationship between the returns on three transportation stocks and the Standard and Poor's 500 index.

$$R_{AMR} = 0.03 + 0.9(R_M), \quad \sigma_{AMR} = 0.10$$
$$R_{UAL} = 0.05 + 1.1(R_M), \quad \sigma_{UAL} = 0.14$$
$$R_{CF} = 0.04 + 1.2(R_M), \quad \sigma_{CF} = 0.12$$

1.   In a portfolio of only one of these transportation stocks, which is most risky?

    a.   stock *AMR*
    b.   stock *UAL*
    c.   stock *CF*
    d.   Both stocks *UAL* and *AMR* are equally risky.
    e.   none of the above

2. Which stock adds the most risk to a well-diversified portfolio?

    a. stock *UAL*
    b. stock *AMR*
    c. stock *CF*
    d. Both stocks *UAL* and *CF* are equally risky.
    e. none of the above

3. If the return on the Standard and Poor 500 index is 0.11, the expected returns on stocks *UAL* and *CF*

    a. are 0.129 and 0.171.
    b. are 0.129 and 0.172.
    c. are 0.171 and 0.160.
    d. cannot be determined from the above information.
    e. none of the above

(The following data apply to Self-Test Problems 4 through 7.)

Consider the following sample of historical returns for FMC corporation and the S&P 500 Index.

Year	FMC Corporation	S&P 500 Index
1988	.12	.09
1989	.05	.08
1990	-.04	-.02
1991	.13	.10
1992	.14	.20

4. The mean and variance for the sample of historical returns for FMC corporation are

    a. 0.08 and 0.0058.
    b. 0.07 and 0.0058.
    c. 0.09 and 0.0076.
    d. 0.08 and 0.0046.
    e. none of the above

5. The mean and variance for the sample of historical returns for the S&P 500 Index are

   a. 0.09 and 0.0024.
   b. 0.08 and 0.0049.
   c. 0.07 and 0.0052.
   d. 0.09 and 0.0061.
   e. none of the above

6. The covariance between FMC corporation and the S&P 500 Index is

   a. 0.0042.
   b. 0.0208.
   c. 0.0052.
   d. 0.0086.
   e. none of the above

7. The OLS regression estimates of the FMC corporation intercept and beta coefficient are

   a. 0.0035 and 0.85.
   b. 0.0048 and 0.25.
   c. 0.0100 and 0.85.
   d. 0.0092 and 0.93.
   e. none of the above

ANSWERS TO SELF-TEST QUESTIONS

1.	error term		12.	True
2.	beta		13.	True
3.	ordinary least squares		14.	True
4.	unsystematic		15.	False
5.	False		16.	True
6.	False		17.	False
7.	True		18.	False
8.	True		19.	False
9.	True		20.	True
10.	False		21.	d
11.	False		22.	b

SOLUTIONS TO SELF-TEST PROBLEMS

1. b. UAL is the most risky stock if it is the only stock in the portfolio because UAL has the largest standard deviation of 0.14.

2.   c.   In a well-diversified portfolio, beta is the appropriate measure of risk for a stock. Stock CF is the most risky because its beta of 1.2 is the highest.

3.   e.   The expected return on stock UAL is:
$$E(r_{UAL}) = 0.05 + 1.1\ (0.11) = 0.171$$
The expected return on stock CF is:
$$E(r_{CF}) = 0.04 + 1.2\ (0.11) = 0.172$$

4.   a.   The mean return for the FMC Corporation is:
$$E(r_i) = (0.12 + 0.05 - 0.04 + 0.13 + 0.14)/5 = 0.08$$
The variance of return for FMC Corporation is:

$$\sigma_i^2 = \frac{(0.12-0.08)^2+(0.05-0.08)^2+(-0.04-0.08)^2+(0.13-0.08)^2+(0.14-0.08)^2}{(5-1)} = 0.0058$$

5.   d.   The mean return for the S&P 500 is:
$$E(r_M) = (0.09 + 0.08 - 0.02 + 0.10 + 0.20)/5 = 0.09$$
The variance of return for the S&P 500 is:

$$\sigma_M^2 = \frac{(0.09-0.09)^2+(0.08-0.09)^2+(-0.02-0.09)^2+(0.10-0.09)^2+(0.20-0.09)^2}{(5-1)} = 0.0061$$

6.   c.   The covariance of the FMC Corporation and the S&P 500 Index is:
$$\sigma_{iM} = [(0.12 - 0.08)(0.09 - 0.09) + (0.05 - 0.08)(0.08 - 0.09)$$
$$+ (-0.04 - 0.08)(-0.020 - 0.09) + (0.13 - 0.08)(0.10 - 0.09)$$
$$+ (0.14 - 0.08)(0.20 - 0.09)]/(5-1) = 0.0052$$

7.   a.   The beta coefficient of the FMC Corporation is:

$$\beta_i = \frac{\sigma_{iM}}{\sigma_M^2} = \frac{0.0052}{0.0061} = 0.85$$

The intercept term from the OLS regression is:
$$\alpha_i = E(r_i) - \beta_i\ E(r_M)$$
$$= 0.08 - (0.85)(0.09) = 0.0035$$

CHAPTER 9

CAPITAL MARKET EQUILIBRIUM: THE CAPITAL ASSET PRICING MODEL

OVERVIEW

This chapter describes the capital asset pricing model (CAPM) and illustrates the following: (1) how the CAPM is derived and interpreted, (2) the differences between the capital market line (CML) and the CAPM, (3) why systematic risk is the relevant portion of risk to be price, (4) how empirical tests are conducted for the CAPM and the results of the tests, and (5) criticisms of the CAPM.

OUTLINE

I.   The capital asset pricing model was developed by Sharpe, Lintner, and Mossin. The CAPM explains the relationship between security expected returns and their risks in terms of the means and standard deviations.

     A.   Assumptions used in the development of the CAPM are:

          1.   Investors are risk averse.
          2.   Investors make investment decisions on the basis of expected return and the standard deviation of return.
          3.   Investors behave in a normative sense and desire to hold a portfolio that lies along the efficient frontier.
          4.   Investors can borrow or lend unlimited amounts at the risk-free rate.
          5.   All investments are perfectly divisible.
          6.   Investors have homogeneous expectations about the return distribution of securities.
          7.   There are no imperfections or frictions such as transaction costs and taxes in the market.
          8.   There is no uncertainty about expected inflation.
          9.   Capital markets are in equilibrium.

     B.   Lending and borrowing at the riskless rate—Combining any risky portfolio with a riskless asset produces a linear relation between their expected returns and standard deviations. In order to maximize expected return for a given level of risk, investors will choose portfolios on the straight line drawn from the riskless rate to the portfolio *M*, which is tangent to the efficient frontier curve. All investors should choose the same portfolio *M* because that portfolio, in conjunction with borrowing and lending at the riskless rate, will enable investors to reach the highest expected return for their level of desired risk. Since every investor should choose to hold portfolio *M*, *M* must contain all securities in the market and is called the market portfolio. Each security in *M* should have a relative market weight proportional to the total market value of *M*.

C.   The capital market line (CML)—With the ability to lend and borrow at the riskless rate, in conjunction with an investment in the market portfolio, the old curved efficient frontier is transformed into a new linear efficient frontier called the capital market line. The CML expresses the equilibrium pricing relationship between expected return and risk for all efficient portfolios lying along the line.

$$E(r_i) = r_f + \{[E(r_M) - r_f]/\sigma_M\}\, \sigma_i \qquad\qquad (9.6)$$

D.   The capital asset pricing model (CAPM)—For individual securities or inefficient portfolios, the CML equation cannot be used. Instead, the capital asset pricing model is used which expresses the equilibrium relation between securities' expected returns and their betas risk, which is the security return covariance with the market portfolio.

$$E(r_i) = r_f + [E(r_M) - r_f]\beta_i \qquad\qquad (9.8)$$

The CAPM says that unsystematic risk should not be priced, since investors can costlessly diversify away this risk. The CAPM can be used to identify overpriced and underpriced securities. Graphically, any securities that lie below the CAPM line are overpriced because their expected returns are not high enough to compensate investors for the systematic risk. Securities that have negative betas should have an expected return less than the riskless rate because of their ability to reduce portfolio risk due to the negative covariance.

E.   The CML v. the CAPM—Even though the CML is appropriate only for well-diversified portfolios, for both the CAPM and CML, the appropriate measure of risk is systematic since, for well-diversified portfolios, total and systematic risk are the same.

II.   Empirical tests of the capital asset pricing model.

A.   Ex-ante expectations and ex-post tests—All the variables in the capital asset pricing model equation are ex-ante expectations of what investors believe will be the values for these variables in the future. However, almost all empirical tests of the CAPM have used ex-post, realized returns data. Using ex-post or historical data to test the model assumes that actual data is suitable proxies for expectations.

B.   Testing the CAPM—First, individual stock betas are estimated, using the single-index model. Because individual stock betas are usually estimated with some errors, most empirical studies group securities into portfolios in order to test the CAPM. Second, by regressing average returns against portfolio betas over different time periods, one can determine whether the coefficients of the regression conform to the CAPM theory. According to the CAPM, the average value of the intercept term should equal the risk-free rate. The slope coefficient should be positive indicating that the relation between beta and expected return is positive.

C.   Empirical results—A thorough empirical study by Fama and MacBeth shows that over the long run, there is a significant and positive relation between average return and beta. However, the intercept term is generally greater than the risk-free rate. Furthermore, there is no evidence of the existence of unsystematic risk or any significant nonlinearity in the regression.

D.   Criticisms of the CAPM by Richard Roll—Because the true market portfolio cannot be measured, it is not possible to determine empirically whether the true market portfolio is mean-variance efficient. Thus the CAPM cannot be tested. Furthermore, performance measures based on the CAPM are likely to be misleading.

VOCABULARY REVIEW

normative approach
capital asset pricing model
homogeneous expectations
lending portfolio
borrowing portfolio
separation theorem
market portfolio
capital market line

risk premium
ex-ante expectation
ex-post data
mean-variance efficiency
beta
capital market theory
systematic risk

SELF-TEST QUESTIONS

Definitional

1.   The CAPM assumption of _____ _____ indicates that investors completely agree about the return distribution for each security.

2.   Combinations of a long position in a risky portfolio with a long position in the riskless asset are called _____ portfolios.

3. The portfolio which consists of all risky securities in the market is called the _____ portfolio.

4. The separation theorem of the CAPM separates _____ and _____decisions.

5. The _____ _____ line is a linear efficient frontier passing from the risk-free security through the market portfolio.

6. The equilibrium relationship between securities' expected returns and their covariances with the market portfolio is called the _____ _____ _____ _____.

7. The systematic risk of a stock is generally referred to as _____ in the CAPM.

Conceptual

8. An increase in a stock's variance of returns will always increase its beta.

    a. True   b. False

9. The borrowing portfolio in the CAPM requires a short sale of the risk-free security.

    a. True   b. False

10. The market portfolio consists of risky and risk-free securities.

    a. True   b. False

11. According to the CAPM, the only combination of risky assets which will be considered by all investors is the market portfolio.

    a. True   b. False

12. The capital market line relates the expected return on a security to the beta of the security.

    a. True   b. False

13. The CAPM assumes that all investors are risk-averse.

    a. True   b. False

14. According to the CAPM, both the capital market line and the security market line (CAPM) are linear.

   a.   True   b.   False

15. The capital market line sets the relationship between expected return and risk for all securities and portfolios.

   a.   True   b.   False

16. A negative beta security has a lower expected return than the risk-free security.

   a.   True   b.   False

17. An example of a source of unsystematic risk is

   a.   a strong economic recovery.
   b.   a labor strike.
   c.   a decline in the risk-free rate.
   d.   a high level of unemployment.
   e.   all of the above

18. Which is *not* an assumption of the capital asset pricing model?

   a.   risk aversion
   b.   homogeneous expectations
   c.   perfect capital market
   d.   the law of one price
   e.   all of the above

19. Which of the following statements is *false* with regard to the CAPM?

   a.   If the market portfolio is not efficient, the CAPM is inappropriate as a measure of expected return.
   b.   The capital market rewards investors for taking only systematic risk.
   c.   The market portfolio contains systematic and unsystematic risks.
   d.   The CAPM is a single-factor model.
   e.   All investors hold the market portfolio.

SELF-TEST PROBLEMS

1. If the risk-free rate is .04, the beta on AT&T is 1.1, and the market risk premium $(E(r_m) - r_f)$ is .07, what is the expected return on AT&T stock?

   a. 0.117
   b. 0.073
   c. 0.110
   d. 0.113
   e. none of the above

(The following data apply to Self-Test Problems 2 and 3.)

Suppose four stocks represent all the risky securities in the market and all the pairwise covariances are zero.

Stock	Total Value	Standard Deviation
IBM	$50	0.05
3M	$40	0.15
GM	$60	0.10
GE	$50	0.20

2. What is the standard deviation of the market portfolio?

   a. 0.4456
   b. 0.0668
   c. 0.1170
   d. 0.1514
   e. none of the above

3. If the risk-free rate is 0.03, the expected return on the market portfolio is 0.11, and the beta of GE is 1.2, what is the expected return of GE?

   a. 0.162
   b. 0.112
   c. 0.126
   d. 0.132
   e. none of the above

4.   Suppose that you are given the following information:

Portfolio	$E(r_i)$	σ_i
A	0.16	0.10
B	0.14	0.09
C	0.11	0.07
D	0.09	0.06
E	0.08	0.04
r_f	0.03	—

Your finance professor tells you that each of portfolios A, B, C, D, and E is on the efficient frontier and that one of them is the market portfolio. If the risk-free rate is 0.03, which portfolio is the market portfolio?

a.   portfolio A
b.   portfolio B
c.   portfolio C
d.   portfolio D
e.   portfolio E

(The following data apply to Self-Test Problems 5 and 6.)

John Soros is in charge of the Portfolio Management Division of Dean Witter. As part of his responsibilities, he must perform an annual review of the recommendations made to him regarding portfolios being considered for the coming year. He is currently considering the portfolios whose expected returns, beta coefficients, and standard deviations are given below:

Portfolio	$E(r_i)$	β_i	σ_i
1	0.08	1.3	0.088
2	0.18	2.0	0.124
3	0.16	1.4	0.101
4	0.07	0.6	0.009
5	0.13	1.2	0.065
S&P 500 Index	0.10	1.0	0.050
Treasury bills	0.03	0.0	0.000

5. According to the CAPM, the following portfolios are underpriced:

   a. portfolios 1 and 4
   b. portfolio 1
   c. portfolios 1, 2, and 3
   d. portfolios 2, 3, and 5
   e. All the portfolios are underpriced.

6. According to the CML, the following portfolios lie below the CML:

   a. portfolios 4 and 5
   b. portfolios 1, 2, and 4
   c. portfolios 1, 2, and 3
   d. portfolios 2 and 4
   e. All the portfolios lie below the CML.

ANSWERS TO SELF-TEST QUESTIONS

1.	homogeneous expectations	11.	True
2.	lending	12.	False
3.	market	13.	True
4.	investing, financing	14.	True
5.	capital market	15.	False
6.	capital asset pricing model	16.	True
7.	beta	17.	b
8.	False	18.	d
9.	True	19.	c
10.	False		

SOLUTIONS TO SELF-TEST PROBLEMS

1. a. The expected return of AT&T stock is:
   $$E(R) = 0.04 + (1.1)(0.07) = 0.117$$

2. b. The weights of IBM, 3M, GM, and GE are, respectively:
   0.25, 0.20, 0.30, 0.25.
   Because all of the pairwise covariances are zero, there are no covariance terms needed to compute the variance of the market portfolio.

The variance of the market portfolio is:
$$\sigma_M^2 = (0.25)^2(0.05)^2 + (0.20)^2(0.15)^2 + (0.30)^2(0.10)^2 + (0.25)^2(0.20)^2 = 0.004456$$
The standard deviation of the market portfolio is:

$$\sigma_M = \sqrt{0.004456} = 0.0668$$

3. c. The expected return of GE is:
$$E(R) = 0.03 + (0.11 - 0.03)(1.2) = 0.126$$

4. a. The market portfolio is the portfolio which maximizes the slope of the ray drawn from the risk-free rate to the efficient frontier:
Maximize $[E(r_M) - r_f]/\sigma_M$,   where $r_f = 0.03$

Portfolio	Slope
A	1.300
B	1.222
C	1.143
D	1.000
E	1.250

A is the market portfolio.

5. d. The CAPM relation is given by the following equation:
$$E(r_i) = r_f + [E(r_M) - r_f]\,\beta_i$$
$$= 0.03 + (0.10 - 0.03)\,\beta_i$$
$$= 0.03 + 0.07\,\beta_i$$
Inserting the value of β_i for each of the portfolios, we calculate the CAPM required return. We then compare the CAPM required return to $E(r_i)$ for each portfolio to determine if the portfolio is underpriced, overpriced, or correctly priced.

Portfolio	$E(r_i)$	CAPM required return	Relationship
1	0.08	.121	$E(r_i) < \text{CAPM}$
2	0.18	.170	$E(r_i) > \text{CAPM}$
3	0.16	.128	$E(r_i) > \text{CAPM}$
4	0.07	.072	$E(r_i) < \text{CAPM}$
5	0.13	.114	$E(r_i) > \text{CAPM}$

Portfolios 2, 3, and 5 are underpriced.

6.   c.   The CML relation is given by the following equation:

$$E(r_i) = r_f + \{[E(r_M) - r_f]/\sigma_M\}\,\sigma_i$$
$$= [0.03 + (0.10 - 0.03)/0.05]\,\sigma_i$$
$$= 0.03 + 1.4\,\sigma_i$$

Inserting the value of σ_i for each of the portfolio, we calculate the CML required return. We then compare the CML required return to $E(r_i)$ for each portfolio to determine which of the portfolios lies below the CML.

Portfolio	$E(r_i)$	CML required return	Relationship
1	0.08	0.153	$E(r_i) < \text{CML}$ ✓
2	0.18	0.204	$E(r_i) < \text{CML}$ ✓
3	0.16	0.171	$E(r_i) < \text{CML}$ ✓
4	0.07	0.043	$E(r_i) > \text{CML}$
5	0.13	0.121	$E(r_i) > \text{CML}$

Portfolios 1, 2, and 3 lie below the CML.

CHAPTER 10

EXTENSIONS TO THE CAPITAL ASSET

PRICING MODEL

OVERVIEW

This chapter describes extensions of the capital asset pricing model (CAPM) and illustrates the following: (1) to understand what a zero beta portfolio is and why the zero beta version of the CAPM is a viable alternative pricing model to the basic CAPM; (2) to recognize that taxes are an important consideration in the pricing of securities; (3) to discover why skewness is important to investors; (4) to recognize the similarities and differences between the CAPM and the arbitrage pricing model (APT); (5) to determine what factors, other than systematic risk, are important in the pricing of securities; and (6) to become aware of the problems that exist for the testing of the APT.

OUTLINE

I. Relaxing the assumptions of the CAPM.

   A. Alternative borrowing and lending conditions:

      1. Differential borrowing and lending rates—Because the borrowing rate differs from one investor to another, each investor will have a different CML and CAPM. Thus, there is no unique equilibrium pricing relation that exists for all securities across all investors.

      2. No riskless asset—Eliminating the existence of a riskless asset is termed the zero beta version of the CAPM. A zero beta portfolio is a portfolio with no systematic risk, but it has unsystematic risk. The equilibrium pricing relation states that the expected return on any security is a linear function of the expected returns on the market and the minimum-variance zero beta portfolio.

      3. Riskless lending but no riskless borrowing—Investors can buy the riskless asset but cannot short-sell it. For investors who want to combine the riskless asset with some risky efficient portfolio, the optimal portfolio is the one that is at the tangency point from a ray drawn from the riskless asset and the curved efficient frontier. This portfolio is not the same as the market portfolio. The equilibrium relation between expected return and

beta for all risky securities in the market portfolio is given by the zero beta version of the model. However, combinations of the riskless asset and the tangency portfolio are not described by this equilibrium relation.

B.   Divisibility of assets—When assets are not perfectly divisible, the CML and CAPM relations become dashed segments rather than one continuous line. Each line segment represents a portfolio containing only full, nonfractional shares.

C.   Homogeneous expectations and investment horizons—Different return distribution forecasts and investment horizons by investors produce different efficient frontiers and different CMLs and CAPMs. Thus, there is no unique equilibrium pricing relation for all investors.

D.   Market imperfections:

    1.   Transaction costs—The presence of transaction costs would place bands around the existing CML and CAPM lines. Between these bands it would not be profitable for investor to trade in order to revise their existing portfolios.

    2.   Taxes—Since investors choose optimal portfolios on the basis of their after-tax return, the efficient frontier may vary from investor to investor because of different effective tax rates. Thus, the CML and CAPM relation tends to vary among investors, depending on their marginal tax rates.

E.   Reliance on expected returns and variances—Relaxing this assumption means that investors not only focus on the first two moments of securities return distribution but also the third moment, the skewness. Although many researchers found skewness to be important in the pricing of assets, the topic is still an unresolved issue.

II.   The arbitrage pricing model: theoretical development.

A.   Arbitrage arguments, assumptions, and the arbitrage pricing model—The arbitrage investors must sell at the same price. Otherwise, investors will arbitrage away the difference. The APT does not require some of the strong assumptions pertaining to the CAPM. The APT states that security returns are a linear function of many factors, which represent systematic influences on individual security returns. For example, a factor might be the market portfolio or changes in expected inflation.

Unlike the CAPM, the APT provides no direction as to what the factors are. The return on any asset i can be expressed as a linear function of a set of M factors or indexes:

$$r_i = \beta_{i0} + \beta_{i1}I_1 + \beta_{i2}I_2 + \beta_{i3}I_3 + ... + \beta_{iM}I_M + \varepsilon_i \qquad (10.7)$$

where

i_i = return on asset i

β_{i0} = expected return on asset i if all the indexes have a return of zero.

β_{ij} = sensitivity of asset i's return to the jth index

I_j = value of the jth index

ε_i = random error term for asset i

B. An illutration of the arbitrage pricing model—The text illustrates the theory using a three factor model.

III. The arbitrage pricing model: empirical tests.

A. Methodology and issues—The technique most commonly used to test the APT is called factor analysis. Factor analysis determines, simultaneously, a specific set of β_{ij}'s and I_j's such that the covariance of residual returns among the securities used in the sample is as small as possible.

B. Hypotheses: because the specific factors in the APT are not specified, a priori hypothesis regarding the magnitude of the risk premiums cannot be stated. However, there are three hypotheses that are of interest in empirical tests of the model. First, the influence of the factors should be significant in explaining the differences among different asset returns. Second, only systematic influence should be important in the pricing equation. Third, the APT requires that each security sample be priced with the same set of factors.

C. Empirical tests—Important factors identified by empirical tests are: industrial production, the risk premium as measured by the yield differential between long-term corporate bonds and government bonds, unexpected inflation, and oil prices. In general, the empirical evidence regarding the APT is ambiguous because the results are highly dependent on the time period analyzed and the sample size.

VOCABULARY REVIEW

zero beta portfolio
minimum-variance zero beta portfolio
homogeneous expectations
coskewness coefficient
skewness
third moment

arbitrage pricing theory
factor
factor analysis
factor loading
risk premium

SELF-TEST QUESTIONS

Definitional

1. A portfolio which has no systematic risk and some unsystematic risk is called a _____ _____ portfolio.

2. The third moment of the security return distribution is the _____ _____.

3. The security's systematic skewness is referred to as the _____ _____ _____ coefficient.

4. The _____ _____ theory states that asset prices are determined through an arbitrage relation.

5. According to the APT, the systematic influences on individual security returns are called _____.

6. The yield differential between long-term corporate bonds and government bonds is a type of _____ _____.

Conceptual

7. The lending rate can be lower or higher than the borrowing rate.

   a.   True   b.   False

8. The zero beta version of the CAPM is a viable alternative pricing model to the basic CAPM.

   a.   True   b.   False

9.   Riskless lending but no riskless borrowing implies that investors can buy Treasury bills but they cannot sell them.

      a.   True   b.   False

10.   Even with heterogeneous expectations, there is a unique equilibrium pricing relation that exists for all securities across all investors.

      a.   True   b.   False

11.   A zero beta portfolio has unsystematic risk.

      a.   True   b.   False

12.   The presence of taxes would place bands around the existing CML and CAPM relations.

      a.   True   b.   False

13.   If the empirically derived CAPM intercept term is greater than its theoretical value, it indicates that the model underprices low-risk securities.

      a.   True   b.   False

14.   Most empirical studies find skewness to be important in the pricing of assets.

      a.   True   b.   False

15.   The arbitrage pricing theory is more general than the CAPM because it does not require some of the assumptions pertaining to the CAPM.

      a.   True   b.   False

16.   Factor analysis is the most popular technique used to estimate and test the APT.

      a.   True   b.   False

17.   Most empirical studies show that only one factor is important in the APT.

      a.   True   b.   False

18.   The arbitrage pricing theory offers no direction on determining which or how many factors are relevant.

      a.   True   b.   False

19.   Which of the following is an advantage of the APT over the CAPM?

    a.   APT does not require that stock returns be normally distributed.
    b.   APT does not require homogeneous expectations.
    c.   APT only requires that securities that provide the same payoffs must sell at the same price.
    d.   APT does not require that all investors must own the market portfolio.
    e.   All of the above are advantages of the APT.

20.   Which one of the following is *not* a factor identified by APT empirical studies?

    a.   changes in expected inflation
    b.   risk premium
    c.   market portfolio
    d.   growth rate in industrial production
    e.   All of the above are factors of the APT.

21.   The equilibrium pricing relationship of the CAPM still holds if the following assumptions are relaxed:

    a.   homogeneous expectations
    b.   taxes
    c.   borrowing and lending at the same rate
    d.   existence of a riskless asset
    e.   reliance solely on expected returns and variances

SELF-TEST PROBLEMS

(The following data apply to Self-Test Problems 1 through 3.)

Assume that there are three common factors affecting stocks of GTE and Sears.

Sensitivity to Common Factors

Stock	Factor 1	Factor 2	Factor 3	Riskless Rate
GTE	0.6	1.5	-0.3	0.00
Sears	1.7	1.9	-0.9	0.00

1.	If you expect the risk premiums on factors 1, 2, and 3 are 0.11, 0.08, and 0.03, respectively, what returns do you expect on GTE and Sears?

	a.	0.153 and 0.302
	b.	0.177 and 0.312
	c.	0.177 and 0.275
	d.	0.110 and 0.312
	e.	none of the above

2.	If the actual risk premiums on factors 1, 2, and 3 are 0.10, 0.07, and 0.04, respectively, what returns do you expect on GTE and Sears?

	a.	0.177 and 0.312
	b.	0.177 and 0.275
	c.	0.153 and 0.267
	d.	0.100 and 0.110
	e.	none of the above

3.	The actual return on GTE is 0.13 and on Sears is 0.285. The reason the actual return differs from the expected return is

	a.	the presence of an unsystematic component of the return.
	b.	the result is dependent on the time period analyzed.
	c.	the APT is ambiguous.
	d.	the result is sensitive to the sample size.
	e.	none of the above

(The following data apply to Self-Test Problems 4 and 5.)

Peter Lynch is a private investor who manages his own portfolio. One of Peter's main concerns is the effect of taxes on the required returns of the securities in his portfolio. He is considering the purchases of several stocks in the near future, but prior to making these purchases, he wants to evaluate their desirability using the Litzenberger-Ramaswany tax form of the CAPM. Information relevant to his use of this model is presented below:

Security	$E(r_i)$	β_i	DY_i
1. Abbott Labs	0.12	1.2	0.080
2. Woolworth	0.13	1.5	0.052
3. DuPont	0.11	0.9	0.065
4. Bethlehem Steel	0.16	1.8	0.000
5. Alcoa	0.14	1.1	0.033
6. Coca-Cola	0.08	0.8	0.021
7. S&P 500 Index	0.10	1.0	0.000
8. Treasury bills	0.03	0.0	0.000

4. If the market price on dividend yields (a_1) is 0.20, then according to the Litzenberger-Ramaswany model, the securities which are underpriced are

    a. DuPont and Coca-Cola.
    b. Abbott Labs, Alcoa, and Woolworth.
    c. Bethlehem Steel, Alcoa, and Coca Cola.
    d. All six securities are underpriced.
    e. DuPont, Bethlehem Steel, and Alcoa.

5. The securities which are overpriced are

    a. Abbott Labs, Woolworth, and Coca-Cola.
    b. DuPont, Bethlehem Steel, and Alcoa.
    c. Coca-Cola and Alcoa.
    d. Woolworth and Coca-Cola.
    e. All six securities are overpriced.

(The following data apply to Self-Test Problems 6 and 7.)

Ralph Wanger is a portfolio manager for the Acorn family of mutual funds. Ralph specializes in picking the stocks of small firms that, while very risky, offer considerable return potential. One characteristic of small firms is that their returns are highly (positively) skewed. Ralph has an MBA degree and uses the three-moment CAPM. Information pertaining to five securities and Treasury Bills is given below:

Securities	$E(r_i)$	β_i	DY_i
1. DeVry	0.15	1.3	2.0
2. Checker-Drive-In	0.20	1.7	2.3
3. Zebra Technologies	0.23	2.2	3.1
4. Liqui-Box	0.29	1.3	0.9
5. Wendy	0.14	1.2	1.5
6. Treasury bills	0.03	0.0	0.0

6. If the market price of beta (a_1) and coskewness (a_2) are 0.5 and -0.3, respectively, then according to the three-moment CAPM, the underpriced securities are

    a. DeVry, Wendy, and Liqui-Box.
    b. DeVry, Checker-Drive-In, and Zebra Technologies.
    c. Wendy.
    d. Liqui-Box and Wendy.
    e. All five securities are underpriced.

7. The overpriced securities are

a. Liqui-Box and Wendy.
b. Devry, Checker-Drive-In, and Zebra Technologies.
c. Liqui-Box and DeVry.
d. Wendy and Zebra Technologies.
e. All five securities are overpriced.

ANSWERS TO SELF-TEST QUESTIONS

1.	zero beta		12.	False
2.	skewness		13.	True
3.	coskewness		14.	True
4.	arbitrage pricing		15.	True
5.	factors		16.	True
6.	risk premium		17.	False
7.	False		18.	True
8.	True		19.	e
9.	True		20.	c
10.	False		21.	d
11.	True			

SOLUTIONS TO SELF-TEST PROBLEMS

1. b. For GTE, $E(r) = 0.6(0.11) + 1.5(0.08) - 0.3(0.03) = 0.177$
   For Sears, $E(r) = 1.7(0.11) + 1.9(0.08) - 0.9(0.03) = 0.312$

2. c. For GTE, $E(r) = 0.6(0.10) + 1.5(0.07) - 0.3(0.04) = 0.153$
   For Sears, $E(r) = 1.7(0.10) + 1.9(0.07) - 0.9(0.04) = 0.267$

3. a. Actual returns are different from expected returns because of unsystematic (or firm-specific) factor returns, which are diversified away in a big portfolio.

4. d. The Litzenberger-Ramaswany (L-R) model is given by:
   $E(r_i) - 0.03 = (0.10-0.03) \beta_i + .20(DY_i - 0.03)$
   $E(r_i) = 0.07 \beta_i + 0.20DY_i + 0.024$
   Inserting the values of β_i and DY for each of the securities, we calculate the Litzenberger-Ramaswany required return. We then compare the L-R required return to $E(r_i)$ for each security to determine if the security is underpriced or overpriced.

Security	$E(r_i)$	L-R Required Return	Underpriced/ Overpriced
1. Abbott Labs	0.12	0.1240	Overpriced
2. Woolworth	0.13	0.1394	Overpriced
3. DuPont	0.11	0.1000	Underpriced
4. Bethlehem Steel	0.16	0.1500	Underpriced
5. Alcoa	0.14	0.1076	Underpriced
6. Coca-Cola	0.08	0.0842	Overpriced

Dupont, Bethlehem Steel, and Alcoa are underpriced.

5.   a.   Abbott Labs, Woolworth, and Coca-cola are overpriced.

6.   b.   The empirical version of the three-moment CAPM is given by:
$$E(r_i) = a_0 + a_1 \beta_i + a_2 \gamma_i$$

where $a_0 = r_f$, $a_1 = 0.5$, and $a_2 = -0.3$
Thus:
$$E(r_i) = 0.03 + 0.5\beta_i - 0.3\gamma_i$$

Investing values of β_i and γ_i for each of the securities, we calculate the three-moment CAPM required return. We then compare the three-moment CAPM required return to $E(r_i)$ for each security to determine if the security is overpriced or underpriced.

Security	$E(r_i)$	Three-moment CAPM Required Return	Underpriced/ Overpriced
1. DeVry	0.15	0.08	Underpriced
2. Checker-Drive-In	0.20	0.19	Underpriced
3. Zebra Tech.	0.23	0.20	Underpriced
4. Liqui-Box	0.29	0.41	Overpriced
5. Wendy	0.14	0.18	Overpriced

DeVry, Checker-Drive-In, and Zebra Technologies are underpriced.

7.   a.   Liqui-Box and Wendy are overpriced.

CHAPTER 11

MATCHING INVESTOR PREFERENCES WITH

PORTFOLIO CHARACTERISTICS

OVERVIEW

This chapter illustrates the following: (1) the concepts of utility and expected utility, (2) the relationship between expected utility of wealth and utility of expected wealth, (3) different mathematical functions that can be used to describe utility functions for risk-averse investors, (4) the difference between absolute and relative risk aversion, and (5) the first four moments of a return distribution and investors' preferences for different distribution moments.

OUTLINE

I.   The concept of utility and expected utility—Utility refers to the happiness or benefits that an economic good provides. Expected utility is determined by attaching probabilities to the various investment outcomes and multiplying the utility of each outcome by its probability of occurence.

$$E(U) = \sum_{i}^{n}(U_i)(p_i) \qquad (11.1)$$

II.   Justification for the expected utility criterion—Investors typically analyze portfolios in terms of expected utility, not expected value. In the "St. Petersburg paradox" example, Bernoulli expressed utility for the participant using a log utility funciton.

$$U(W) = \ln(W) \qquad (11.2)$$

The solution to the St. Petersburg paradox is based on the observation that most people are risk-averse.

III.   Assumptions about investor behavior—Traditionally, a mathematical function is used to describe the relationship between an investor's wealth and the utility of that wealth. Once the utility function has been described, the different derivatives of the function tell us the investor's attitude toward changes in wealth.

IV.   Attitudes of investors toward risk.

   A.   Risk-loving attitude—The risk lover is a gambler who will enter a fair game of chance paying a price greater than the expected value of the gamble. For the risk lover, the utility function of wealth is convex.

   B.   Risk-neutral attitude—A risk-neutral person is indifferent toward risk and toward a fair gamble. The utility function of a risk-neutral investor can be graphed as a straight line.

   C.   Risk-averse attitude—It is assumed that most investors are risk-averse. The utility function of a risk-averse investor is concave, indicating that the utility added from each additional unit of wealth diminishes as wealth increases.

V.   Functions used to describe risk-averse investors.

   A.   Log utility function—If $U(W)$ equals $\ln(W)$, then $U_1(W)$ equals $1/W$ and is always positive, meaning that more is always preferred to less, and $U^2(W)$ equals $-1/W^2$ and is always negative, implying risk aversion over all ranges of wealth.

   B.   Quadratic utility function:
$$U(W) = \alpha + \beta W - CW^2 \tag{11.3}$$

   Note that α is unrestricted in sign, while β and C must be greater than zero. β has a positive sign attached to it, while C's sign is negative. One limitation of the quadratic utility function is that it can be defined only for a restricted range of outcomes up to the point $W_x = \beta/2C$.

   C.   Power and exponential functions: with the power function, utility function is expressed as wealth to a fractional power.
$$U(W) = -\alpha + W^{1-\beta} \quad (0<\beta<1) \tag{11.4}$$

   The exponential function takes the form of the following equation, in which e is raised to a power involving W:
$$U(W) = 1 - e^{-\beta W} \quad (\beta>0) \tag{11.5}$$

VI.   Absolute and relative risk aversion: investors' perception of risk can be measured in terms of absolute amount of dollars they would invest in risky assets, termed absolute risk aversion (ARA), or in the percentage of wealth they invest in risky assets, called relative risk aversion (ARA).

A.   Absolute risk aversion: investors who increase their dollar investment in risky assets as their wealth increases are said to exhibit decreasing absolute risk aversion. ARA can be measured as the ratio of $U^2(W)$ to $U^1(W)$.

$$ARA(W) = -\frac{U^2(W)}{U^1(W)} \tag{11.6}$$

B.   Relative risk version: measures the investor's attitude toward the percentage of wealth to invest in risky assets. Relative risk aversion can be expressed as:

$$RRA(W) = -\frac{WU^2(W)}{U^1(W)} \tag{11.7}$$

VII.   Selecting the optimal portfolio.

A.   Portfolio selection under quadratic utility: because a quadratic utility function requires only $E(r)$ and σ^2 of a risky asset to calculate $E(U)$, the problem of selecting from among a variety of alternative investments is simplified.

B.   Portfolio selection: the general case.

1.   Moments of the return distribution—The first moment of a return distribution is the mean. The second moment about the mean is the variance. The third moment is the skewness, which is calculated exactly like the variance except that the deviations are cubed rather than squared. Skewness is a measure of the asymmetry of the distribution. For a negatively skewed distribution, the skewness is less than zero because the extreme returns that are smaller than the mean outweigh the ones that are larger. The fourth moment about the mean is the kurtosis, which is the sum of the deviations from the mean taken to the fourth power. Higher positive values of kurtosis indicate more peakedness in the distribution. Flat distributions exhibit lower values of kurtosis.

2.   Investor's preferences for return distribution moments—Measurement of risk becomes more complex if the return distribution is not normal, because the measure of risk must incorporate all higher moments of the distribution. It is assumed that investors like positive skewness and all odd-numbered moments of the distribution and that investors dislike even-numbered moments beginning with the variance.

3.   Return distributions using discrete and continuous returns—Empirical evidence indicates that large portfolios of stocks exhibit normal distribution of returns over certain time periods and have positive or negative skewness

111

over other periods. Individual stock return distributions typically are positively skewed. Much of the asymmetry in security and portfolio returns can be eliminated by calculating returns as a continuously compounded rate of return rather than the discrete period return.

4. Solving for expected utility—If the possible returns are continuous rather than discrete, the calculation of expected utility is complicated and requires the use of a Taylor series expansion.

VIII. Relationship between utility theory and portfolio analysis—Portfolio theory and asset valuation principles are based either on the premise that asset return distributions are normal or on the assumption that the investor's utility function is quadratic. For stock and bond portfolios, the normality assumption usually is appropriate enough to allow mean-variance analysis to hold. However, for portfolios composed of stocks, bonds, and options, which possess positive skewness, higher moments of the distribution should be considered.

VOCABULARY REVIEW

utility
expected utility
certainty equivalent
risk premium
risk-averse
quadratic utility function
absolute risk aversion
risk-neutral

relative risk aversion
distribution moment
skewness
coefficient of skewness
kurtosis
coefficient of kurtosis
discrete return

SELF-TEST QUESTIONS

Definitional

1. Happiness or welfare derived from an economic asset is called _____.

2. The dollar value that will make the investor indifferent between accepting the risky gamble and taking the guaranteed outcome with no risk is called the _____ _____.

3. A _____ _____ investor is indifferent toward risk and toward a fair gamble.

4. For a _____ _____ investor, the utility added from each additional unit of wealth diminishes as wealth increases.

5.	If investors have _____ _____ risk aversion, the dollar amount they invest in risky securities increases as their wealth increases.

6.	The third moment about the mean is the _____.

7.	_____ is the fourth moment about the mean.

8.	When the logarithms of the discrete returns are normally distributed, the return are _____ _____ distributed.

Conceptual

9.	For a risk-averse investor, the utility function that graphs utility as a function of wealth is convex.

	a.	True		b.	False

10.	If the investor's expected utility of wealth is less than the utility of expected wealth, then the investor is risk-averse.

	a.	True		b.	False

11.	The risk premium is the difference between the expected value of the gamble and its certainty equivalent.

	a.	True		b.	False

12.	Risk aversion means that the utility added from each additional unit of wealth increases as wealth increases.

	a.	True		b.	False

13.	The quadratic utility function implies risk aversion over all ranges of wealth.

	a.	True		b.	False

14.	Relative risk aversion measures the investor's attitude toward the dollar investment in risky assets.

	a.	True		b.	False

15. The quadratic utility function implies that the investor has increasing relative risk aversion.

    a.   True   b.   False

16. The quadratic utility function allows expected utility to be expressed in terms of only the expected return and the variance.

    a.   True   b.   False

17. If the skewness is positive, the mean is smaller than either the mode or the median.

    a.   True   b.   False

18. The skewness is calculated exactly like the variance except that the deviations are cubed rather than squared.

    a.   True   b.   False

19. If a distribution is normal, the mean, median and mode are equal.

    a.   True   b.   False

20. A normal distribution has zero skewness and zero kurtosis.

    a.   True   b.   False

21. If the return distribution is non-normal, all moments of the distribution should be considered when determining investor uility.

    a.   True   b.   False

22. The mean-variance framework may give misleading results when used to analyze portfolios of stocks and options.

    a.   True   b.   False

23. Which of the following is *not* an implication of the quadratic utility function?

    a.   It allows expected utility to be expressed in terms of only the expected return and the variance of return.
    b.   It is appropriate to evaluate options and futures contracts.
    c.   The quadratic utility function can be defined only for a restricted range of wealth.
    d.   The intercept term of the quadratic utility function is unrestricted in sign.
    e.   all of the above

24.   Which of the following statements is *most* correct?

    a.   For a risk-neutral investor, the graph portraying utility as a function of wealth is concave.

    b.   For the log, power and exponential functions have constant relative risk aversion.

    c.   If the expected utility of wealth is greater than the utility of expected wealth, then the investor is risk-loving.

    d.   A risk-neutral investor is willing to pay a risk premium to avoid a fair gamble.

    e.   Most investors prefer a negatively skewed distribution of returns.

SELF-TEST PROBLEMS

(The following data apply to Self-Test Problems 1 and 2.)

Consider the following information for investment A and B:

A			B	
Probability	Return		Probability	Return
0.50	0.16		0.50	0.20
0.50	0.06		0.50	0.02

Thomas O'Connor has a utility function of the form:
$U(r) = 10 + 60r + 20\ r^2$

1.   Calculate the expected utility of each investment for Thomas.

    a.   20.112 and 22.800
    b.   16.892 and 17.004
    c.   13.692 and 11.208
    d.   16.892 and 13.672
    e.   none of the above

2.   Calculate the utility of expected return for each investment.

    a.   16.892 and 17.004
    b.   16.842 and 13.672
    c.   15.913 and 16.842
    d.   16.842 and 16.842
    e.   none of the above

(The following data apply to Self-Test Problems 3 through 5.)

Consider the following values for two investments:

A				B		
Probability	Wealth	Utility		Probability	Wealth	Utility
0.30	20	3.7514		0.20	19	3.6514
0.40	15	2.5653		0.60	14	2.9432
0.30	9	1.7105		0.20	5	1.0237

3.   The expected wealths, $E(W)$, for investments A and B are

   a.   14.7 and 15.1.
   b.   15.8 and 14.7.
   c.   14.7 and 13.2.
   d.   14.1 and 13.2.
   e.   none of the above

4.   The expected utility values for investments A and B are

   a.   2.6647 and 2.4008.
   b.   2.7009 and 2.8152.
   c.   2.5103 and 2.6107.
   d.   2.6647 and 2.7009.
   e.   none of the above

5.   Which investment should the investor choose? Why?

   a.   investment B; because it has the highest expected utility
   b.   investment A; because it has the highest expected utility
   c.   either investment A or B; because the investor is indifferent
   d.   investment A; because it has the largest wealth value
   e.   investment B, because it is less risky

ANSWERS TO SELF-TEST QUESTIONS

1.	utility	13.	False
2.	certainty equivalent	14.	False
3.	risk-neutral	15.	True
4.	risk-averse	16.	True
5.	decreasing absolute	17.	False
6.	skewness	18.	True
7.	Kurtosis	19.	True
8.	log normally	20.	False
9.	False	21.	True
10.	True	22.	True
11.	True	23.	b
12.	False	24.	c

SOLUTIONS TO SELF-TEST PROBLEMS

1. b. For investment A:
$$U(0.16) = 10 + 60(0.16) + 20(0.16)^2 = 20.112$$
$$U(0.06) = 10 + 60(0.06) + 20(0.06)^2 = 13.672$$
The expected utility of investment A is:
$$E[U(A)] = 0.5(20.112) + 0.5(13.672) = 16.892$$

For investment B:
$$U(0.20) = 10 + 60(0.20) + 20(0.20)^2 = 22.800$$
$$U(0.02) = 10 + 60(0.02) + 20(0.02)^2 = 11.208$$
The expected utility of investment B is:
$$E[U(B)] = 0.5(22.800) + 0.5(11.208) = 17.004$$

2. d. The expected returns for investments A and B are:
A: $E(r) = 0.5(0.16) + 0.5(0.06) = 0.11$
B: $E(r) = 0.5(0.20) + 0.5(0.02) = 0.11$
Since both investments have the same expected return of 0.11, the utility of expected return for both investment is:
$$U[E(r) = 10 + 60(0.11) + 20(0.11)^2 = 16.842$$

3. c. The expected wealth of investment A is:
$$E(W_A) = 0.3(20) + 0.4(15) + 0.3(9) = 14.7$$
The expected wealth of investment B is:
$$E(W_B) = 0.2(19) + 0.6(14) + 0.2(5) = 13.2$$

4. d. The expected utility of investment A is:
$$E(U_A) = 0.3(3.7514) + 0.4(2.5653) + 0.3(1.7105) = 2.6647$$

The expected utility of investment B is:
$$E(U_B) = 0.2(3.6514) + 0.6(2.9432) + 0.2(1.0237) = 2.7009$$

5.   a.   The investor should choose investment B to maximize expected utility.

CHAPTER 12

EVALUATING INVESTMENT PERFORMANCE

OVERVIEW

This chapter shows you the following: (1) how to measure returns using time-weighting and dollar-weighting schemes, (2) the portfolio evaluation measures developed from the CAPM by Sharpe, Treynor, and Jensen, (3) how to decompose the portfolio manager's performance between selectivity and timing, and (4) two measures that can be used to identify dominant assets—the geometric mean and stochastic dominance.

OUTLINE

I.   Calculating returns.

      A.   Dollar-weighted rate of return—The dollar-weighted rate of return is an internal rate of return of cash flows that occur during the measurement period. To quote a return on an annualized basis, either an arithmetic or geometric "annualizing" calculation is used.

      B.   Time-weighted returns—The portfolio's value just before a cash flow occurs is used as the numerator in the return calculation. The denominator is the sum of the portfolio's value in the previous period and the cash inflow. The rate of return is not weighted by the dollars invested, but is combined with returns over the following periods to get an annualized rate of return. The time-weighted return is probably more accurate to evaluate investment managers because the dollar-weighted return is sensitive to large intra-period cash flows over which the fund manager has no control. Empirical evidence indicates that professional money managers, on average, do not earn a return equal to the S&P 500 over previous 3-, 5-, or 10-year periods.

II.   Performance measures from industry—Investors who place their money with professional fund managers expect them to add value to their portfolio. The value that is added is a return superior to that of an unmanaged stock portfolio like the S&P 500 Index, and it is achieved through (1) selectivity, that is, choosing stocks that do better than average for their level of risk, and through (2) timing, that is, being in stocks that rise and out of stocks that decline.

III.   Risk-adjusted performance measures.

A.   Treynor measure is the portfolio's excess return per unit of systematic risk. The Treynor measure can be used to rank portfolios because the higher its value, the better the portfolio's performance.

$$T_i = \frac{\bar{r}_i - \bar{r}_f}{\beta_i} \qquad (12.3)$$

where

T_i = the Treynor measure

$\bar{r}_i$ = the realized average return on the security

$\bar{r}_f$ = the average riskless rate

β_i = the portfolio's beta

B.   Jensen measure: is the vertical-axis intercept in the regression of excess portfolio returns against excess market returns. For the market portfolio, the Jensen measure is zero. Any portfolios with Jensen measures statistically greater than zero out-perform the market, whereas those with negative Jensen measures underperform the market, on a risk-adjusted basis.

$$J_i = \bar{r}_i - [\bar{r}_f + (\bar{r}_M - \bar{r}_f)\beta_i] \qquad (12.6)$$

where:

J_i = the Jensen measure

$\bar{r}_M$ = the average return for the market

C.   Sharpe's measure is the portfolio's excess return per unit of total risk.

$$S_i = \frac{\bar{r}_i - \bar{r}_f}{\sigma_i} \qquad (12.7)$$

where

S_i = the Sharpe measure
σ_i = the standard deviation of the portfolio

The Sharpe measure is appropriate when the portfolio comprises the investor's entire wealth in financial assets. On the other hand, the Jensen and Treynor measures are appropriate when the portfolio represents only a portion of the investor's wealth.

IV. Decomposing portfolio performance using the CAPM—The overall excess return of a portfolio can be decomposed into its selectivity and risk components. Selectivity can be decomposed further into net selectivity and diversification, whereas risk can be decomposed into the fund manager's risk portion and the investor's risk portion.

V. Problems of CAPM-based measures.

A. Defining the market portfolio—The theoretical market portfolio consists of all economic assets, including stocks, bonds, real estate, precious metals, and so on. However, no market index is available that contains all economic assets.

B. Violation of the assumptions about riskless borrowing—If the borrowing rate is higher than the lending rate, the Sharpe, Treynor, and Jensen measures lead to a bias toward identifying low-risk portfolios as superior.

C. Application of the ex-ante CAPM model to past data—The CAPM is developed in an ex-ante context, and may not be appropriate to evaluate the past performance of financial assets.

D. Portfolios with nonnormal return distributions—Application of any CAPM-derived performance measure will not provide the proper evaluation of performance for these portfolios.

VI. Wealth maximization criterion—The wealth maximization criterion indicates that an investor, regardless of his utility function, should choose the portfolio that has the greatest expected geometric mean return over time in order to maximize expected terminal wealth. Portfolios that are mean-variance efficient may have low geometric mean returns, and portfolios with high geometric means may not be mean-variance efficient. However, if portfolio returns are log-normally distributed, the portfolio that maximizes the geometric mean return will lie on the efficient frontier.

A. The geometric mean—The geometric mean is the Tth root of the product of T terms:

$$G = \left[\prod_{t=1}^{T} (1 + r_t) \right]^{\frac{1}{T}} - 1 \qquad (12.12)$$

121

B. Risk and the geometric mean—Because the geometric mean calculation incorporates the variance in the distribution of returns, its value will always be less than the arithmetic mean.

C. The wealth maximization criterion and utility functions—The wealth maximization criterion is equivalent to maximizing the expected value of a log utility function.

VII. Rules of stochastic dominance—Stochastic dominance is a preference-ordering technique that requires only minor assumptions about the shape of the investor's utility function and no assumptions about the asset's return distribution. The rule divides investments into two categories: a dominant or efficient group and an inefficient group. Stochastic dominance is not popular because it involves more complex mathematics and requires significantly more data than CAPM derived measures.

VOCABULARY REVIEW

dollar-weighted return	wealth maximization criterion
time-weighted return	geometric mean
selectivity	efficiency criterion
market timing	stochastic dominance
Treynor measure	first-degree stochastic dominance
Jensen measure	second-degree stochastic dominance
Sharpe measure	third-degree stochastic dominance

SELF-TEST QUESTIONS

Definitional

1. The internal rate of return of the cash flows that occur during a period is called the _____ _____ return.

2. The _____ measure is the portfolio's excess return per unit of systematic risk.

3. According to the CAPM, the portfolio that represents all economic assets is called the _____ portfolio.

4. The _____ _____ criterion indicates that investors should choose the portfolio that maximizes expected terminal wealth.

5. An _____ _____ criterion identifies the smallest efficient set given assumptions about the investor's utility function.

6.   _____ _____ stochastic dominance assumes only that investors prefer more to less.

7.   _____ _____ stochastic dominance assumes that investors must possess decreasing absolute risk aversion.

Conceptual

8.   The time-weighted return is considered more representative of the fund manager's performance, because it is not influenced as much by cash flows over which the fund manager has no control.

       a.   True   b.   False

9.   When dealing with a time series of returns, the geometric annualizing calculation is appropriate because it reflects the compounding of interest and principal through time.

       a.   True   b.   False

10.   Empirical evidence indicates that professional money managers on average outperform the Standard and Poor's 500.

       a.   True   b.   False

11.   The Treynor measure considers total risk as the appropriate risk measure for a portfolio.

       a.   True   b.   False

12.   Portfolios with Jensen measures statistically greater than zero may be judged to have outperformed the market.

       a.   True   b.   False

13.   The Jensen measure is suitable for ranking portfolios with different risks.

       a.   True   b.   False

14.   If the portfolio is well diversified, the Sharpe, Treynor, and Jensen measures will give consistent indicators compared to the market.

       a.   True   b.   False

15. The Jensen and Sharpe measures are appropriate to evaluate portfolios that represent only a portion of the investor's total wealth.

a. True   b. False

16. Selectivity can be decomposed into two components: net selectivity and diversification.

a. True   b. False

17. The CAPM-based measures are appropriate to evaluate portfolios of options and futures contracts.

a. True   b. False

18. The wealth maximization criterion indicates that the investor should choose the portfolio that maximizes expected terminal wealth.

a. True   b. False

19. The wealth maximization criterion argues that the investor should choose the portfolio that has the greatest expected arithmetic mean return over time.

a. True   b. False

20. The higher the variability in the per-period returns, the greater the divergence between the arithmetic and geometric mean values.

a. True   b. False

21. The arithmetic return is best used to describe the central tendency of a return distribution at a point in time.

a. True   b. False

22. The objective of the wealth maximization criterion is to maximize the expected utility of an investor.

a. True   b. False

23. Portfolios that are mean-variance efficient must have high geometric mean returns.

a. True   b. False

24. An optimal efficiency criterion is one that identifies the smallest efficient set given assumptions about the investor's utility preferences.

   a.   True   b.   False

25. Second-degree stochastic dominance assumes only that investors prefer more to less.

   a.   True   b.   False

26. Stochastic dominance requires a lot more data than the Sharpe, Treynor, and Jensen measures in order to evaluate portfolio performance.

   a.   True   b.   False

27. Which of the following is *not* a technique to evaluate investment performance?

   a.   the Treynor measure
   b.   the Sharpe measure
   c.   stochastic dominance
   d.   the Beta measure
   e.   the Jensen measure

28. Which of the following statements is *most* correct?

   a.   Second-degree stochastic dominance includes the restriction that the investor must possess decreasing absolute risk aversion.
   b.   The wealth maximization criterion is identical to the strategy of maximizing the geometric-mean return of the investment.
   c.   The arithmetic return is appropriately applied to a time series of returns.
   d.   The CAPM-based measures can be used to evaluate portfolios whose return distributions are skewed.
   e.   The overall excess return of a portfolio can be decomposed into net selectivity and diversification.

29. Which of the following is a problem of the portfolio performance measures based on the CAPM?

   a.   defining the market portfolio
   b.   portfolios with nonnormal return distributions
   c.   violation of the assumptions about riskless borrowing
   d.   application of the ex-ante CAPM model to past data
   e.   all of the above

SELF-TEST PROBLEMS

(The following data apply to Self-Test Problems 1 through 3.)

Suppose USX and AMR have the following rates of return:

YEAR	USX RETURN	AMR RETURN
1989	0.19	0.12
1990	-0.08	0.07
1991	-0.05	-0.06
1992	0.10	-0.11
1993	0.14	0.18

1.   The arithmetic average annual returns for USX and AMR are

   a.   0.06 and 0.05.
   b.   0.06 and 0.04.
   c.   0.075 and 0.05.
   d.   0.05 and 0.06.
   e.   none of the above

2.   The standard deviations for USX and AMR are

   a.   0.1190 and 0.1219.
   b.   0.1190 and 0.1090.
   c.   0.1065 and 0.1191.
   d.   0.1065 and 0.1090.
   e.   none of the above

3.   The geometric average returns for USX and AMR are

   a.   0.0546 and 0.0342.
   b.   0.0600 and 0.0400.
   c.   0.0580 and 0.0375.
   d.   0.0646 and 0.0442.
   e.   none of the above

4. The Fidelity Magellan mutual fund had an average return of 0.20 in the past ten years. The beta of the fund is 1.20. During the same period, the risk-free rate averaged is 0.03, and the average annual rate of return of the market portfolio was 0.11. The Jensen measure of the Fidelity Magellan fund is

   a. 14.0.
   b. 9.0.
   c. 7.4.
   d. Not enough information is given to compute the Jensen measure.
   e. none of the above

(The following data apply to Self-Test Problems 5 through 7.)

Consider the following risk and return measures:

Portfolio	Return	Standard Deviation	Beta
A	0.114	0.19	0.90
B	0.182	0.24	1.60
C	0.163	0.14	0.88
D	0.202	0.30	1.20
Market	0.131	0.16	1.00
r_f	0.040	0.00	0.00

5. The Treynor measures of portfolios A, B, and C, are, respectively,

   a. 0.0822, 0.0888, and 0.1350.
   b. 0.0888, 0.1398, and 0.1350.
   c. 0.0822, 0.0888, and 0.1398.
   d. 0.1350, 0.1398, and 0.0910.
   e. none of the above

6. The Sharpe measures of portfolios B, C, and D, are, respectively,

   a. 0.5917, 0.8786, and 0.5400.
   b. 0.8786, 0.5400, and 0.5688.
   c. 0.3895, 0.5917, and 0.8786.
   d. 0.5917, 0.8786, and 0.5688.
   e. none of the above

7. The Jensen measures of portfolios A, B, and C, are, respectively,

    a. -0.0079, -0.0036, and 0.0528.
    b. -0.0036, 0.0000, and 0.0429.
    c. -0.0036, 0.0429, and 0.0528.
    d. -0.0079, -0.0036, and 0.0429.
    e. none of the above

8. By the Sharpe measure, which portfolios overperform the market?

    a. portfolios B and C
    b. portfolios B, C, and D
    c. portfolios B and D
    d. Only portfolio C overperforms the market.
    e. All four portfolios overperform the market.

9. Rank the performance of the portfolios and the market by the Jensen measure.

    a. B, A, M, D, C
    b. D, C, M, B, A
    c. D, C, M, A, B
    d. M, D, C, B, A
    e. none of the above

ANSWERS TO SELF-TEST QUESTIONS

1.	dollar-weighted		16.	True
2.	Treynor		17.	False
3.	market		18.	True
4.	wealth maximization		19.	False
5.	optimal efficiency		20.	True
6.	First-degree		21.	True
7.	Third-degree		22.	False
8.	True		23.	False
9.	True		24.	True
10.	False		25.	False
11.	False		26.	True
12.	True		27.	d
13.	False		28.	b
14.	True		29.	e
15.	False			

SOLUTIONS TO SELF-TEST PROBLEMS

1. b. The arithmetic average return for USX is:
$$(0.19 - 0.08 - 0.05 + 0.10 + 0.14)/5 = 0.06$$
The arithmetic average return for AMR is:
$$(0.12 + 0.07 - 0.06 - 0.11 + 0.18)/5 = 0.04$$

2. a. The variance of USX is:
$$[(0.19-0.06)^2 + (-0.08-0.06)^2 + (-0.05-0.06)^2 + (0.10-0.06)^2 + (0.14-0.06)^2]/4 = 0.01415$$

The standard deviation for USX is the square root of 0.01415, which is 0.1190.

The variance of AMR is:
$$[(0.12-0.04)^2 + (0.07-0.04)^2 + (-0.06-0.04)^2 + (-0.11-0.04)^2 + (0.18-0.04)^2]/4 = .01485$$
The standard deviation for AMR is the square root of 0.01485, which is 0.1219.

3. a. The geometric average return for USX is:

$$\sqrt[5]{(1.19)(0.92)(0.95)(1.1)(1.14)} - 1 = \mathbf{0.0546}$$

The geometric average return for AMR is:

$$\sqrt[5]{(1.12)(1.07)(0.94)(0.89)(1.18)} - 1 = \mathbf{0.0342}$$

4. c. Solving this equation for the Jensen measure:

$$\bar{r}_p - \bar{r}_f = J + \beta(\bar{r}_M - \bar{r}_f)$$

$$20 - 3 = J + 1.2(11 - 3)$$
$$17 = J + 9.6$$
$$J = 7.4$$

5.   c.   The Treynor measure equation is:

$$T_i = (\bar{r}_i - \bar{r}_f)/\beta_i$$

$$T_A = (0.114 - 0.04)/0.90 = 0.0822$$
$$T_B = (0.182 - 0.04)/1.6 = 0.0888$$
$$T_C = (0.163 - 0.04)/0.88 = 0.1398$$
$$T_D = (0.202 - 0.04)/1.2 = 0.1350$$
$$T_M = (0.131 - 0.04)/1.0 = 0.0910$$

6.   a.   The Sharpe measure equation is:

$$S_i = (\bar{r}_i - \bar{r}_f)/\sigma_i$$

$$S_A = (0.114 - 0.04)/0.19 = 0.3895$$
$$S_B = (0.182 - 0.04)/0.24 = 0.5917$$
$$S_C = (0.163 - 0.04)/0.14 = 0.8786$$
$$S_D = (0.202 - 0.04)/0.30 = 0.5400$$
$$S_M = (0.131 - 0.04)/0.16 = 0.5688$$

7.   d.   The Jensen measure equation is:

$$J_i = \bar{r}_i - [\bar{r}_f + (\bar{r}_M - \bar{r}_f)\beta_i]$$

$$J_A = 0.114 - [0.04 + (0.091)(0.9)] = -0.0079$$
$$J_B = 0.182 - [0.04 + (0.091)(1.6)] = -0.0036$$
$$J_C = 0.163 - [0.04 + (0.091)(0.88)] = 0.0429$$
$$J_D = 0.202 - [0.04 + (0.091)(1.2)] = 0.0528$$

8.   a.   Portfolios B and C outperform the market because they have higher Sharpe measures than that of the market.

9.   b.   The ranking of the portfolios and the market by the Jensen measure is: D, C, M, B, and A.

CHAPTER 13

BOND VALUATION AND INTEREST RATE THEORY

OVERVIEW

This chapter shows you the following: (1) how to value bonds and determine a bond's price, (2) various measures to compute a bond's yield, (3) the concept of interest on interest in evaluating a bond's long-run return, (4) the factors that determine the levels of bond yields and why yields may vary from one bond to another, and (5) the term structure of interest and various theories used to explain it.

OUTLINE

I.   Bond valuation

    A.   Present value theory (a review)—Determining the value of a bond, or any asset, requires the estimation of four things: (1) the cash flows, (2) the timing of the cash flows, (3) the estimated holding period, and (4) the required return.

    B.   Bond valuation with annual coupons—The price of a bond is the present value of all cash flows (annual coupon interest payments and the maturity value), discounted at the required yield.

    C.   Bond valuation with semiannual coupons—When the bond pays coupons on a semiannual basis, the number of periods to maturity must be doubled, because there are *2n* compounding periods, and the discount rate and the annual coupon payment must be halved.

$$P_0 = \sum_{t=1}^{2n} (C_t/2)/(1 + i/2)^t + M_{2n}/(1 + i/2)^{2n} \qquad (13.3)$$

    where

        $C_t/2$ = semi-annual coupon payment
        $2n$ = total number of semi-annual coupon payments
        $i/2$ = semi-annual required yield

D. Relationships between a bond's price, coupon, yield, and maturity:

1. The price of a bond will change in a direction opposite to the change in the required yield.
2. When the coupon rate equals the required yield, the bond price will equal its par value of $1,000.
3. When the coupon rate is greater (less) than the required yield, the bond will sell at a premium (discount) to its par value.
4. As a bond selling at par approaches maturity, the portion of value from the principal (coupon) becomes larger (smaller). At maturity, the value of the bond equals its principal value of $1,000.
5. Holding the yield constant, the price of a bond will move toward its par value as the bond approaches maturity.

II. Measuring the yield and return on a bond.

A. Bond yield measures:

1. Coupon rate is the percentage of total annual income a bond will pay relative to the par value.
2. Current yield is the annual interest income divided by the market price of the bond.
3. Yield to maturity is the discount rate that makes the present value of the cash flows equal to the price of the bond today. This rate is the internal rate of return for the bond.
4. Yield to call is computed to the first call date and represents the discount rate that equates the present value of the cash flows, coupons plus call price, with today's bond price.

B. Measuring a bond's total return and the importance of reinvesting—The holding period yield return measures the total return on an one-period basis. It has two components: the return of the principal and the interest income. When moving from a single-period return to a long-run compounded return, the interest earned on the interest income must be considered. This interest-on-interest component is the major component of the total return of a long-term bond.

III.   Determinants of bond yields and yield spreads: the required return or annual yield to maturity for a bond, i, can be expressed as the sum of three components: the real rate of return, the rate of expected inflation, and the risk premium.

$$i = i_f + i_I + i_p \qquad\qquad (13.8)$$

where

i_f = real rate of return
i_I = rate of expected return
i_p = risk premium

A.   Expected inflation and the real rate of interest—The interest rate on a riskless bond is the sum of the real rate of interest and the expected inflation rate. Consequently, all bond yields, both risky and riskless, should compensate investors for these two effects.

B.   Risk premiums and yield spreads:

1.   Term to maturity—The term premium is the difference between the yield on a short-term bond and a longer-term bond with identical characteristics. The yield curve shows the relation between yield and maturity. Historically, the upward-sloping yield curve is most common.

2.   Credit risk—Credit risk measures the risk that the issuer will default. Credit risk evaluations are conducted by recognized organizations such as Moody's and Standard & Poor's, which provide bond ratings. The top four classification groups (AAA, AA, A, and BBB) are investment grade bonds. Bonds with rating below BBB are called junk bonds or high-yield bonds.

3.   Tax considerations qualified illiquidity—Because the interest income from qualified municipal bonds is exempt from federal income taxes, the yields on these securities will contain a negative tax premium to reflect this advantage. Generally speaking municipal bonds are less liquid and, have a smaller market, and generally take longer to buy and sell than comparable corporate and Treasury securities. Therefore, the yields on municipal bonds contain a positive liquidity premium.

4.   Indenture provision—Certain indenture provisions, such as deferred call provision, can influence the risk premium present in bonds. Callable bonds not only create uncertainty about the cash flows, but they also force the investor to reinvest the proceeds of a callable bond when interest rates have declined, which is the period that bonds are called.

5.   Foreign exchange risk—Because the cash flow from a foreign bond depends on the exchange rate that exists between dollars and the foreign currency at the time the cash flow is received, foreign bond yields will contain a foreign exchange risk premium.

133

IV.   The term structure of interest rates—The relation between yield and maturity on securities that differ only in the length of time to maturity is the term structure of interest rates.

    A.   Drawing the term structure—The most direct way to draw the term structure is to use a sample of U.S Treasury STRIPS, which are default-free zero coupon bonds.

    B.   Spot rates, forward rates, and theories of the term structure.

        1.   Spot rates and forward rates—The term structure reflects spot rates of interest for a given maturity. Implied in the term structure of spot rates at any point in time is a set of forward rates.

        2.   Expectation theory—The term structure is formed by the expectations of investors regarding future interest rates. This theory assumes that the forward rate implied in today's term structure equals what the market expects this rate to be.

        3.   Liquidity premium theory—Liquidity premium theory claims that a liquidity premium must be offered in the yield of long-term securities to induce investors to buy them. Otherwise, investors would prefer to invest in short-term securities.

        4.   Market segmentation theory—The behavior of borrowers and lenders determines the relation between yield and maturity. Large institutional investors may have certain preferences for either short-term or long-term securities. Therefore, the shape of the yield curve will reflect the demand by these investors for their preferred segment of the market.

VOCABULARY REVIEW

present value concept	Fisher effect
annuity	risk premium
semiannual coupon	term premium
zero coupon bond	investment grade bond
coupon rate	junk bond
current yield	negative tax premium
yield to maturity	deferred call provision
internal rate of return	spot rate
fully compounded rate of return	forward rate
term structure of interest rates	nominal yield
yield to call	expectation theory
yield spread	liquidity premium theory
real rate of return	market segmentation theory

SELF-TEST QUESTIONS

Definitional

1. An _____ represents a stream of equal payments over a period of time, with equal time between each payment.

2. The percentage of total annual income that a bond will pay relative to the par value is called the _____ _____.

3. The _____ _____ is the annual interest income divided by the current market price of a bond.

4. The discount rate that makes the present value of the bond's cash flows equal to the bond price is called the _____ _____ _____.

5. All bonds with a rating below investment grade are called _____ _____.

6. The relationship between yield and maturity on securities that differ only in the length of time to maturity is called the _____ _____ of interest rates.

7. The _____ theory states that the forward rate implied in today's term structure is equal to the expected spot rate.

Conceptual

8. The economic value of any asset is the present value of all expected future cash flows.

    a. True   b. False

9. The price of a bond will always move in a direction opposite to the change in the required yield.

    a. True   b. False

10. When the coupon rate is less than the required yield, the bond will sell at a premium.

    a. True   b. False

11. Holding the yield constant, the price of a bond will move toward its par value as the bond approaches maturity.

   a.   True   b.   False

12. The coupon rate for a bond is the most widely used yield measure.

   a.   True   b.   False

13. The current yield is the required yield that makes the present value of the cash flows equal to the bond's price.

   a.   True   b.   False

14. The yield to call is also referred to as the internal rate of return for the bond.

   a.   True   b.   False

15. The Fisher effect accounts for the expected inflation and the real rate of return in establishing a bond's yield.

   a.   True   b.   False

16. All bonds issued by the same company must have the same bond rating.

   a.   True   b.   False

17. Once a bond rating is established, it cannot be changed for a year.

   a.   True   b.   False

18. The call provision allows the issuer to redeem the bond at a predetermined price before maturity.

   a.   True   b.   False

19. The liquidity premium theory states that the forward rate implied in the term structure is equal to the expected spot rate.

   a.   True   b.   False

20. The market segmentation theory is strongly supported by empirical evidence.

   a.   True   b.   False

21. The liquidity premium theory usually predicts an upward-sloping yield curve.

   a.   True   b.   False

22. Which of the following is the best yield measure of a bond?

   a.   current yield
   b.   yield to maturity
   c.   coupon rate
   d.   nominal yield
   e.   none of the above

23. Which of the following statements is *most* correct?

   a.   There is an inverse relationship between a bond's price and its required yield.
   b.   When the coupon rate is less than the required yield, a bond's price will be selling at a discount.
   c.   As a bond selling at par approaches maturity, the principal portion becomes larger.
   d.   The yield to maturity is the fully compounded rate of return that an investor expects to earn from the time the bond is purchased until maturity.
   e.   All of the above statements are correct.

24. Which of the following is *not* an implication of the liquidity premium theory?

   a.   A risk premium must be offered in the yield of long-term securities to induce investors to buy them.
   b.   The yield curve is usually upward sloping.
   c.   The longer the time to maturity, the larger the liquidity premium.
   d.   The forward rate implied in the term structure is equal to the expected spot rate in the future.
   e.   All of the above statements represent implications of the liquidity premium theory.

SELF-TEST PROBLEMS

1. What is the yield to maturity of the Exxon bond with an annual coupon rate of 6 percent, a par value of $1,000, a time to maturity of 10 years, when the current price of the bond is $929.72?

    a. 6.00 percent.
    b. 6.45 percent.
    c. 7.00 percent.
    d. 7.30 percent.
    e. none of the above

2. The yield to maturity on a ten-year bond is 6 percent, the yield to maturity on a eleven-year bond is 6.5 percent. The implied forward rate on a one-year bond at the start of year eleven is

    a. 6.25 percent.
    b. 11.63 percent.
    c. 8.53 percent.
    d. 9.74 percent.
    e. none of the above

3. Assume the following yields on U.S. Treasury STRIP securities at the present time:

Time to Maturity	Yield
1 year	3.00%
2 years	3.10%
3 years	3.25%

    Assume a pure expectations theory, the implied forward rate on a one-year bond at the start of year 2 is

    a. 3.20 percent.
    b. 3.10 percent.
    c. 3.54 percent.
    d. 3.25 percent.
    e. none of the above

(The following data apply to Self-Test Problems 4 and 5.)

Tom Vu is a portfolio manager in the fixed-income division of Harris Associates. He is contemplating the purchase of some additional bonds for the portfolios that he manages. Two new issues that he is considering are detailed below:

Issuer	Semi-annual Coupon Rate	Maturity (Years)	Semi-annual Yield to Maturity	First Call Date	First Call Price
Home Depot	4.5%	14	4%	5	105
Kroger	4.0%	20	5%	7	104

4. In deciding which bond to purchase, Tom plans to conduct a preliminary pricing and yield analysis. Assume semi-annual coupon payments, compute the price of Home Depot and Kroger bonds.

   a. $1,083.34 and $851.52
   b. $1,020.56 and $828.36
   c. $1,054.41 and $903.27
   d. $1,083.34 and $828.36
   e. none of the above

5. The annual yields to call for the Home Depot and Kroger bonds are

   a. 7.8 percent and 11 percent.
   b. 8.0 percent and 10 percent.
   c. 7.8 percent and 12 percent.
   d. 3.9 percent and 6 percent.
   e. none of the above

ANSWERS TO SELF-TEST QUESTIONS

1.	annuity	13.	False
2.	coupon rate	14.	False
3.	current yield	15.	True
4.	yield to maturity	16.	False
5.	junk bonds	17.	False
6.	term structure	18.	True
7.	expectations	19.	False
8.	True	20.	False
9.	True	21.	True
10.	False	22.	b
11.	True	23.	e
12.	False	24.	d

SOLUTIONS TO SELF-TEST PROBLEMS

1.   c.   Using the trial-and error method along with Equation 13.3 and tables B.1 and B.2, assume that $i = 7\%$:

$929.72 = $60(PV factor of an annuity at 7%, 10 years)
+ 1000(PV factor at 7%, 10 years)
= $60(7.0236) + 1000(0.5083)
= $929.72

Therefore, the yield to maturity of the Exxon bond is 7 percent.

2.   b.   The implied forward rate at the start of year eleven is:
$[(1.065)^{11}/(1.06)^{10}] - 1 = 1.1163 - 1 = 0.1163$ or 11.63%

3.   a.   The implied forward rate at the start of year 2 is:
$[(1.031)^2/(1.03)] - 1 = 1.0320 - 1 = 0.0320$ or 3.20%

4.   d.   The prices for the Home Depot and Kroger bonds can be found with the use of Equation 13.3 and Tables B.1 and B.2.

$$P_0 = \sum_{t=1}^{2n} \frac{(C_t/2)}{(1+i/2)^t} + \frac{M_{2n}}{(1+i/2)^{2n}}$$

The price of the Home Depot bond is:

$$P_0 = \sum_{t=1}^{28} \frac{\$45}{(1+0.04)^t} + \frac{\$1,000}{(1+0.04)^{28}}$$

$$= \$45(16.6631) + \$1,000(0.3335) = \$1,083.34$$

The price of the Kroger bond is:

$$P_0 = \sum_{t=1}^{40} \frac{\$40}{(1+.05)^t} + \frac{\$1,000}{(1+.05)^{40}}$$

$$= \$40(17.1591) + \$1,000(0.1420) = \$828.36$$

5.   c.   To find the semi-annual yield to call ($i/2$), equation 13.7 is used:

$$P_0 = \sum_{t=1}^{2nc} \frac{(C_{t/2})}{(1+i/2)^t} + \frac{CP}{(1+i/2)^{2nc}}$$

The equation for the Home Depot bond is:

$$\$1,083.34 = \sum_{t=1}^{10} \frac{\$45}{(1+i/2)^t} + \frac{\$1,050}{(1+i/2)^{10}}$$

Using the trial-and-error method, for $i/2 = 4.0\%$
$$P_0 = \$45(8.1109) + \$1,050(0.6756)$$
$$= \$364.99 + \$709.38$$
$$= \$1,074.37$$

Hence, the semi-annual yield to call for the Home Depot bond is approximately 3.9 percent. The annual yield to call is approximately 7.8 percent.
The equation for the Kroger bond is:

$$\$828.36 = \sum_{t=1}^{14} \frac{\$40}{(1+i/2)^t} + \frac{\$1,040}{(1+i/2)^{14}}$$

For $i = 6.0\%$
$$P_0 = \$40(9.2950) + \$1,040(0.4423)$$
$$= \$371.80 + \$459.99$$
$$= \$831.79$$

Hence, the semi-annual yield to call for the Kroger bond is approximately 6 percent. The approximate annual yield to call is 12 percent.

CHAPTER 14

MANAGING FIXED-INCOME PORTFOLIOS

OVERVIEW

This chapter describes how investors can manage bond portfolios and gives you a better understanding of the following: (1) what is bond price volatility and the factors that cause bond prices to change, (2) duration and its measurements, and (3) several of the more popular passive and active bond management strategies.

OUTLINE

I.   Properties of bond price volatility—Bond price volatility is the sensitivity of a bond price to changes in the required yield on the bond.

   A.   Property 1—There is an inverse, nonlinear relationship between yield to maturity and the price of a bond.

   B.   Property 2—Holding the term to maturity constant, the lower (higher) the coupon rate, the greater (smaller) the percentage change in price for a given change in required yield.

   C.   Property 3—Holding the coupon rate constant, the longer (shorter) the term to maturity, the greater (smaller) the percentage change in price for a given change in required yield.

   D.   Property 4—Small changes in the required yield produce relatively symmetrical changes in the bond price. That is, bond price increases and decreases that result from small changes in the required yield are approximately equal.

   E.   Property 5—Large changes in the required yield produce unequal changes in the bond's price. A large decrease in the yield will produce a greater increase in the bond's price when compared to the decrease in price that results from an increase in the required yield of the same magnitude.

   F.   Property 6—For a given change in the required yield, the lower (higher) the initial yield, the greater (smaller) the change in a bond's price.

II.   Measuring bond price volatility: duration

    A.   The concept of duration—Duration is the weighted average maturity of a bond's cash flows, where the present values of the cash flows serve as the weights.

    B.   Measuring duration—The most commonly used measure of duration is the Macaulay duration:

        Macaulay duration = D_s
        (in semiannual periods)

$$D_s = (1/P_0) \sum_{t=1}^{2n} (Cashflow_t)[t/(1+i/2)^t] \qquad (14.1)$$

where
Cash flow$_t$ =   semiannual coupon payment or the principal amount
      t =   time period in which the cash flow is received
   $2n$ =   number of semiannual payment periods
   $i/2$ =   semiannual yield to maturity
   P_0 =   current price of the bond

    C.   Properties of duration:

      1.   The duration of a zero coupon bond is always equal to its term to maturity.
      2.   The duration of a coupon bond will be less than its term to maturity, and the relative difference between the two will increase as the term to maturity increases (holding the coupon rate constant).
      3.   For a given term to maturity, the higher (lower) the coupon rate, generally, the smaller (greater) the bond's duration.
      4.   For a given coupon rate, a bond's duration generally increases with its term to maturity.
      5.   For a given term to maturity and coupon rate, generally, the lower (higher) the required yield, the greater (smaller) the duration of the bond.

    D.   Modified duration:
      percent change in price (P_0) $\approx$ [–(Macaulay duration)
          x $(1/(1+i/2))$] x (Change in yield).   (14.4)

    It is common to combine the first two terms in Equation 14.4 into a term called modified duration.

        Modified duration = –Macaulay duration/(1+i/2)   (14.5)

Thus,

$$\text{percent change in price } (P_0) \approx (-\text{Modified duration}) \\ \times (\text{change in yield}) \tag{14.6}$$

The modified duration provides a linkage between yield changes and bond price volatility. Equation 14.6 indicates that the relationship between duration and price volatility is approximate. The greater the convexity of the curvature in the price/yield relationship, the less accurate Equation 14.6 will be in estimating the percentage change in bond's price resulting from a change in the required yield.

III. Managing bond portfolios—Bonds are suitable investment for individuals who have the following objectives: (1) to establish a high level of steady income, (2) to accumulate money to reach a target level of wealth, or (3) to increase total return.

  A. Investing for current income—A common strategy used to achieve this goal is the buy-and-hold approach, where the securities are bought and held until maturity or until the end of the investment horizon of the buyer. The buy-and-hold strategy is a passive approach to bond management. The advantage of this strategy is that there are few expectational requirements regarding future interest rate movements. The disadvantage is that no consideration is given to the total return potential of the portfolio.

  B. Investing to accumulate value—Portfolio strategies that utilize bonds to accumulate value include portfolio dedication, immunization, and contingent immunization.

   1. Portfolio dedication—The objective is to create a bond portfolio that has a cash flow structure that matches the cash flow structure of a stream of liabilities. Under pure cash matching, the cash flows of the portfolio exactly match the required payments for a stream of liabilities. Under cash matching with reinvestment, the portfolio's cash flow plus expected reinvestment income provide the funds at the time when payments are required.

   2. Immunization—The objective is to protect the portfolio value from unforseen changes in future reinvestment rates. A portfolio is immunized if its Macaulay duration is equal to the investment horizon of the investor. Immunization can be used to lock in a certain compounded return, to accumulate a target level of wealth, or to preserve the ability to pay a stream of liabilities. The advantage of immunization over the dedicated portfolio as an approach to accumulate value is its flexibility. It provides the investor with a tool to neutralize the effects of price risk and reinvestment risk. The immunization approach has some limitations. First, the duration of the immunized portfolio requires periodic rebalancing. Second,

it assumes that the term structure is flat. Finally, it assumes that all the shifts in the yield curve are parallel.

3. Contingent immunization—At the beginning, some initial accumulation value of the portfolio is determined. Then the portfolio is managed actively as long as the current value of the portfolio exceeds the predetermined accumulation value. When the portfolio value falls to a minimum acceptable value, it must be immunized at the current market rate to achieve the accumulation goal. This strategy strikes a good balance between passive and active bond management.

C. Investing to increase total returns—The objective is to maximize the total value, given the investor's risk tolerance.

1. Interest rate anticipation—An investor makes a forecast as to how much interest rates will change and in what direction. When interest rates are expected to decline (rise), you increase your investment in long-(short-) duration bonds.

2. Bond swaps—An investor sells a bond and exchanges it with another. In a substitution swap, the securities are similar in all respects except the bond purchased has a higher promised yield to maturity than the bond that is sold. In a pure yield pickup swap, the investor swaps out of a lower-yield bond into a higher-yield bond.

VOCABULARY REVIEW

bond price volatility	reinvestment risk
Macaulay duration	price risk
modified duration	periodic rebalancing
buy-and-hold strategy	contingent immunization
laddered portfolio	safety margin
portfolio dedication	bond swap
pure cash matching	risk-altering swap
immunization	substitution swap
	pure yield pickup swap

SELF-TEST QUESTIONS

Definitional

1. The sensitivity of a bond's price to changes in the required yield is called bond _____ _____ _____.

2. The weighted average maturity of a bond's cash flows is measured by the _____.

3. The _____ duration shows the relation between yield changes and bond price volatility.

4. _____ is a strategy whose objective is to create a portfolio that has a cash flow structure that matches the cash flow structure of a stream of liabilities.

5. A bond portfolio is _____ when its duration is equal to the investor's investment horizon.

6. _____ _____ enables an investor to establish a target accumulation goal, yet it leaves open the opportunity to exceed that objective through active management of the bond portfolio.

7. A _____ _____ is a swap in which securities are similar in all respects except that the bond purchased has a higher promised yield to maturity than the bond that is sold.

8. A swap that changes the market risk of the portfolio or the credit risk is called a _____ _____ swap.

Conceptual

9. There is an inverse linear relationship between yield to maturity and the price of the bond.

   a.   True   b.   False

10. Large changes in the required yield produce symmetrical changes in the bond price.

   a.   True   b.   False

11. For a given change in required yield, the lower the initial yield the greater will be the resultant percentage change in a bond's price.

   a.   True   b.   False

12. The Macaulay duration is sometimes referred to as the modified duration.

   a.   True   b.   False

13. The duration of a coupon bond is always less than its term to maturity.

   a.   True   b.   False

147

14. Duration is a very useful tool in management of bond portfolios because it can be used to immunize the portfolio from changes in yield.

   a.   True   b.   False

15. Empirical evidence indicates that intermediate-term bonds have outperformed long-term bonds over the last 40 years.

   a.   True   b.   False

16. The buy-and-hold strategy is suitable for investors who want to accumulate value over some horizon.

   a.   True   b.   False

17. The buy-and-hold strategy does not require a forecast of future interest rates.

   a.   True   b.   False

18. Pure cash matching is a conservative approach that can be used to construct a dedicated portfolio.

   a.   True   b.   False

19. A portfolio is immunized when its modified duration is equal to the investor's investment horizon.

   a.   True   b.   False

20. Immunization can be used to construct a bond portfolio whose cash flows are used to pay a stream of liabilities.

   a.   True   b.   False

21. Immunization is a passive bond strategy that does not require periodic rebalancing.

   a.   True   b.   False

22. Contingent immunization establishes a minimum acceptable target, but leaves open the opportunity to exceed that objective through active management of the bond portfolio.

   a.   True   b.   False

23. Portfolio dedication is an appropriate strategy for investors who want to increase total returns.

    a.   True   b.   False

24. A substitution swap is an example of a risk-altering swap.

    a.   True   b.   False

25. In a pure yield pickup swap, an investor swaps out of a lower-yield bond into a higher-yield bond without changing the risk of the portfolio.

    a.   True   b.   False

26. Which of the following is a *disadvantage* of the immunization approach?

    a.   Immunization neutralizes the effects of price risk and reinvestment risk.
    b.   Immunization requires periodic rebalancing of the portfolio.
    c.   Immunization is suitable for investors who want to accumulate value.
    d.   Immunization assumes that the yield curve is upward sloping.
    e.   none of the above

27. Which of the following is *not* a portfolio strategy for investors who want to accumulate value over some horizon?

    a.   portfolio dedication
    b.   contingent immunization
    c.   buy-and-hold
    d.   cash matching with reinvestment
    e.   immunization

28. Which of the following statements is *most* correct?

    a.   For a given term to maturity and coupon rate, the higher the required yield, the smaller the duration of the bond.
    b.   A pure yield pickup swap is an example of a risk-neutral swap.
    c.   The Macaulay duration is often referred to as the modified duration.
    d.   Interest rate anticipation is a passive strategy for managing bond portfolio.
    e.   For a given term to maturity, the higher the coupon rate, the greater the bond's duration.

SELF-TEST PROBLEMS

1.   The Kodak bonds have five years remaining to maturity. A 7 percent coupon is paid annually on $1,000 par value. If the yield to maturity is 6 percent, the duration for the Kodak bonds is

    a.   4.40 years.
    b.   5 years.
    c.   4.15 years.
    d.   4.25 years.
    e.   none of the above

2.   AT&T has a bond with four years remaining to maturity. It pays a 7 percent (annual) coupon rate semiannually on $1,000 par value. If the annual yield to maturity is 8 percent, the price of the AT&T bond is

    a. $954.50.
    b. $959.35.
    c. $962.40.
    d. $966.34.
    e.   none of the above

(The following data apply to Self-Test Problems 3 and 4.)

Suppose a Paine Webber bond analyst is evaluating the current holdings of the firm's portfolio:

Bond	Market Value	Duration	Yield to maturity
Bally	$40 million	3 years	8%
AMAX	$50 million	6 years	8%
Grace	$40 million	8 years	8%
GMA	$70 million	10 years	8%

3.   The duration of the Paine Webber bond portfolio is

    a.   7.20 years.
    b.   6.75 years.
    c.   7.10 years.
    d.   not enough information to calculate the duration
    e.   none of the above

150

4.   If the yield to maturity rises to 8.5 percent, and Paine Webber has a horizon date of 7.2 years, the bond analyst should do the following to immunize the portfolio.

   a.   increase the holding of AMAX bonds
   b.   do nothing because the portfolio is already immunized
   c.   increase the holding of Grace and GMA bonds
   d.   increase the holding of Bally and AMAX bonds
   e.   none of the above

(The following data apply to Self-Test Problems 5 through 8.)

Ruth Templeton is a retired lady whose income consists primarily of interest earned on her CDs and Social Security benefits. In the past three years interest rates on CDs have dropped significantly. With several of her CDs maturing in the next few months, Ruth has decided to take the advice of her A.G. Edwards broker and invest her cash in some U.S. Treasury bonds. Her concern, however, is that if interest rates rise, the value of the bonds will fall. Listed below are several Treasury bonds the broker is recommending:

Semi-annual Coupon Rate	Maturity (Years)	Semi-annual Yield to Maturity	Current Price
3%	1	3%	$1,000
3%	10	3%	$1,000
3%	20	3%	$1,000

5.   If the semi-annual yield to maturity suddenly increases by 2 percent, the new prices for these Treasury bonds are

   a. $962.78, $750.77, and $691.80.
   b. $962.78, $750.77, and $656.77.
   c. $974.60, $765.82, and $681.31.
   d. $972.78, $750.77, and $651.92.
   e.   none of the above

6.   The percentage changes in price when the semi-annual yield increases by 2 percent for the three Treasury bonds are

   a.   -3.72 percent, -24.92 percent, -30.82 percent.
   b.   -3.72 percent, -24.92 percent, -34.32 percent.
   c.   -2.54 percent, -23.42 percent, -31.87 percent.
   d.   -2.72 percent, -24.92 percent, -34.81 percent.
   e.   none of the above

7. If the semi-annual yield to maturity suddenly decreases by 1 percent, the new prices for these Treasury bonds are

a. $1,019.45, $1,163.54, and $1,212.42.
b. $1,000.00, $1,094.65, and $1,164.96.
c. $1,014.61, $1,140.51, and $1,219.57.
d. $1,019.45, $1,163.54, and $1,273.57.
e. none of the above

8. The Macaulay duration in terms of years for the Treasury bond with one year left to maturity is

a. 1.971.
b. 0.971.
c. 1.000.
d. 0.985.
e. none of the above

ANSWERS TO SELF-TEST QUESTIONS

1.	price volatility	15.	True
2.	duration	16.	False
3.	modified	17.	True
4.	dedication	18.	True
5.	immunized	19.	False
6.	Contingent immunization	20.	True
7.	substitution swap	21.	False
8.	risk altering	22.	True
9.	False	23.	False
10.	False	24.	False
11.	True	25.	False
12.	False	26.	b
13.	True	27.	c
14.	True	28.	a

SOLUTIONS TO SELF-TEST PROBLEMS

1.   a.

Year	Cash Flow	PV of Cash Flow	(t)*PV of Cash Flow
1	$70	$66.04	$66.04
2	$70	$62.30	$124.60
3	$70	$58.77	$176.31
4	$70	$55.45	$221.80
5	$1,070	$799.61	$3,998.05
		$1,042.17	$4,586.80

The duration of the Kodak bonds (in years) is approximately = $4,586.80/ $1,042.17 = 4.4 years.

2.   d.   Adjusting for semiannual interest payment, the coupon payment becomes $35, the yield to maturity is (8%)/2 = 4%, and the number of periods to maturity is 8. Using Equation 13.3, Tables B.1 and B.2, we get:
P_0 = ($35)(6.7327) + ($1,000)(.7303) = 966.34
The price of the AT&T bond is $966.34.

3.   a.   The duration of the bond portfolio is the weighted average of the duration of individual bonds.
The weights of Bally, AMAX, Grace, and GMA bonds are, respectively: $40/$200 = 0.2, $50/$200 = 0.25, $40/$200 = 0.2, $70/$200 = 0.35.
The duration of Paine Webber's portfolio = 3(0.2) + 6(0.25) + 8(0.2) + 10(0.35) = 7.2 years

4.   c.   The increase in yield to maturity will cause the duration of the Paine Webber portfolio to decline. To remain immunized the bond analyst should increase the holdings of Grace and GMA bonds because they have durations greater than 7.2 years.

5.   b.   The price for each bond can be computed with the use of Equation 13.3 and Tables B.1 and B.2. The new prices when the semi-annual yield increases by 2 percent are: $962.78, $750.77, and $656.77.

$$P_0 = \sum_{t=1}^{2n} \frac{(C_t/2)}{(1+i/2)^t} + \frac{M_{2n}}{(1+i/2)^{2n}}$$

153

6.   b.   The percentage changes in price are:
           ($962.78 − $1000)/$1,000 = −3.72%
           ($750.77 − $1000)/$1,000 = −24.92%
           ($656.77 − $1000)/$1,000 = −34.32%

7.   d.   The price for each bond can be computed with the use of Equation 13.3 and Tables B.1 and B.2. The new prices when the semi-annual yield decreases by 1 percent are:
           $1,019.45, $1,163.54, and $1,273.57.

8.   d.   The Macaulay duration is computed with the use of Equations 14.1 and 14.2:

$$D_S = \frac{1}{P_0} \sum_{t=1}^{2n} (Cash\ Flow) \frac{t}{(1+i/2)^t}$$

$$D_A = \frac{D_2}{2}$$

Semi-Annual Period	Cash Flow	Present Value Factor at 3%	Present Value of Cash Flow	(t) x Present Value of Cash Flow
1	30	0.9709	29.13	29.13
2	1,030	0.9426	970.87	1,941.74
Total			1,000.00	1,970.87

Macaulay duration = D_S = $1,970.87/$1,000 = 1.971
    (semi-annual)

Macaulay duration = D_A = 1.971/2 = 0.985
    (in years)

CHAPTER 15

COMMON AND PREFERRED STOCK VALUATION

OVERVIEW

This chapter illustrates the following: (1) the concept of market value and economic value for a share of stock, (2) the accounting measures of value: par value, book value, liquidation value, and replacement value, (3) the discount dividend model under constant growth and multiple-growth assumptions, (4) the share value comparison using dividend, earnings, and cash flow models, (5) the relationship between the price/earnings ratio and share value, (6) the empirical evidence about the interrelationship between share price, dividends, and earnings, and (7) the effects of overreaction, speculative bubbles, and variance bounds to the valuation process for securities.

OUTLINE

I.   Market value and economic value—Market value is the current quoted price to buy or sell the stock. The economic value is the present value of the cash flows that the share will generate, discounted at the rate of return appropriate for the risk of the company. In a perfectly efficient market the economic value of a share will equal its market value. Most security analysts believe that the market is not perfectly efficient, thus they spend significant resources trying to identify mispriced securities to buy or sell.

II. Accounting measures of stock value.

    A.   Par value is the legal price of the share used in obtaining the corporate charter. Par value is a legal definition which has no economic impact on the firm.

    B.   Book value reflects the value of the common stockholders' account on the firm's balance sheet. Book value is a poor indicator of the economic value of a stock because book value is based on past information and two identical firms can report different book values due to their accounting procedures.

    C.   Liquidation value represents the cash stockholders would receive if the firm discontinues operations, sells its assets, and distributes the proceeds to creditors and stockholders. Liquidation value is the minimum value of a security.

155

D. Replacement value represents the cost of replacing assets of the firm at today's price. Replacement value is hard to determine and is not a good measure of the economic value of a stock.

III. Mathematical models for stock valuation.

A. The discounted dividend model is also called the Gordon model. It describes a stock value as a function of its expected dividends, the market capitalization rate, and the growth rate in dividends. The model can be formulated to consider a single, constant growth rate in dividends over time or multiple growth rates over various future periods. Under the constant growth assumption:

$$P_0 = \sum_{t=1}^{\infty} \frac{D_0(1+g)^t}{(1+k)^t} = D_0 \sum_{t=1}^{\infty} \frac{(1+g)^t}{(1+k)^t} = \frac{D_0(1+g)}{k-g} \qquad (15.6)$$

where
P_0 = today's stock price
g = constant growth rate of dividend
D_0 = current dividend
k = discount rate that is appropriate for the risk class of the stock

B. The discounted earnings model can be developed from the discounted dividend model by making two adjustments: earnings must be defined in an economic rather than an accounting context, and the model must be structured so that earnings are not double counted when they are later paid as dividends.

$$P_0 = \sum_{t=1}^{\infty} \frac{E_t}{(1+k)^t} - \sum_{t=1}^{\infty} \frac{I_t}{(1+k)^t} = \sum_{t=1}^{\infty} \frac{E_t - I_t}{(1+k)^t} \qquad (15.12)$$

where
E_t = accounting earnings during period t
I_t = investment during period t

C. The discounted cash flow model was developed by Modigliani and Miller, who claim that the value of the firm is independent of the manner in which the firm is financed, and dividend policy is irrelevant for the price of the firm's common stock. If earnings are defined as economic earnings, all three models are internally consistent and give the same share valuation.

$$V_t = \sum_{t=1}^{\infty} \frac{E_t - I_t}{(1+k)^t} + 0 = \sum_{t=1}^{\infty} \frac{E_t - I_t}{(1+k)^t} \qquad (15.16b)$$

where

$\quad V_t \;=\;$ value of the stock

$E_t - I_t \;=\;$ yearly cash flow

IV.   Stock valuation and the price/earnings ratio—The P/E ratio is the current price of the stock divided by its most recent annualized earnings. Market professionals view the P/E as one indicator of whether a stock is properly valued compared to other securities and compared to the stock's past values.

V.   Empirical tests of the relationships between stock returns and dividends, earnings, and P/E ratios.

    A.   Dividends and stock prices—Unexpected changes in dividends are, on average, associated with changes in the stock price in the same direction. One study finds that for short holding periods, there is little relationship between dividend yield and stock price. However, when the holding period lengthens to two years, the strength of the relationship between dividend yield and stock price increases.

    B.   Earnings and stock prices—When earnings are in line with the market's expectation, most of the information in the earnings announcement is already impounded in the stock price. However, for firms with surprisingly good or bad earnings, investors take a long time to adjust the valuation of these stocks. This is not consistent with the semistrong-form of market efficiency.

VI.   Stock valuation, overreaction, and speculative bubbles.

    A.   The overreaction hypothesis—This hypothesis assumes that individuals, in responding to new information, tend to overweight recent data and underweight prior data. The empirical evidence regarding the overreaction hypothesis is mixed.

    B.   Speculative bubbles—Investors are convinced that prices, although high today, will be higher tomorrow, and the expectation of future price increases is the only basis for buying the asset.

    C.   Are stock prices too volatile?—Variance bounds represent the relationship that must exist between the variance of market prices and the variance of the true price when the market is efficient. It is argued of that volatility in stock prices is too great to be attributed only to the valuation factors.

VII. Preferred stock represents an equity stock in the firm and has a legal claim on the firm's cash flows and assets. These claims take priority over those of the common stockholders.

A. Characteristics—Preferred stockholders typically have no voting privileges. Most preferred stock is cumulative; that is, if the issuer passes a dividend, then that dividend, along with any subsequent dividends passed, must be paid before common shareholders receive any dividends. Some preferred stock is callable at the option of the issuer. Because twenty percent of the dividends received by one corporation from another are exempt from taxes, the yield on preferred stock is generally less than that on straight debt with the same rating.

B. Valuing preferred stock—The value of a straight preferred stock is the present value of the future dividends, discounted at the market's required return.

$$P_0 = \frac{D_1}{k_p} \qquad (15.21)$$

where

  P_0 = the current market price of the preferred stock
  D_1 = the promised annual dividend one period hence
  k_p = the required return on preferred stock in a given risk class

In valuing convertible preferred stock, investors must consider not only the straight value of the issue, but also the amount of value added by the conversion call option.

C. Adjustable-rate preferred stock has a dividend that is reset quarterly to maintain a specified yield spread above U.S. government securities. For Dutch auction rate preferred stock, the dividend yield is reset every 45 days in an auction process that reduces most of the interest rate risk and default risk.

D. Reasons for buying perferred stock—Investors in preferred stock may be placed in two categories: (1) those who seek stable current income, and (2) those who seek capital gains.

VOCABULARY REVIEW

economic value

noise trader

par value

book value

liquidation value

replacement value

discounted dividend model

Gordon model

retention ratio

growth firm

discounted earnings model

accounting earnings

economic earnings

discounted cash flow model

trailing price/earnings ratio

asymmetric information

overreaction hypothesis

speculative bubble

variance bounds test

preferred stock

cumulative dividend

participating preferred stock

convertible preferred stock

conversion ratio

conversion premium

adjustable-rate preferred stock

dutch auction rate preferred stock

SELF-TEST QUESTIONS

Definitional

1. The _____ value of a share is the present value of the cash flows that the share will generate, discounted at the rate of return appropriate for the risk of the company.

2. _____ is a large number of insignificant events that are not important in the valuation process._____

3. _____ value represents the value of the common stockholders' account as shown on the firm's balance sheet.

4. The discounted dividend model is also called the _____ model.

5. The percentage of earnings retained in the firm is called the _____ _____.

6. A firm which can earn a return greater than the capitalization rate is called the _____ _____.

7. _____ _____ represent the difference between revenues and costs.

8. The current stock price divided by the expected earnings is called the _____ _____ ratio.

9. The _____ hypothesis claims that investors tend to overweight recent data and underweight prior data.

10. A phenomenon in which investors believe that prices, although high today, will be higher tomorrow is called a _____ _____.

11. The _____ _____ research asserts that stock prices are much too volatile to be explained by new information about dividends and earnings.

12. The _____ _____ provision of preferred stock specifies the amount to be retired over time according to the guidelines set forth in the provision.

13. If preferred stockholders share additional dividend increases with common shareholders, the preferred stock has a _____ feature.

14. The number of common shares that each share of a convertible preferred stock can exchanged for is called the _____ _____.

15. A preferred stock whose dividend yield is reset every 45 days in an auction process is called _____ _____ _____ preferred stock.

Conceptual

16. In a perfectly efficient market the economic value of a share is equal to its market value.

   a.   True   b.   False

17. Both noise and information about any individual company occur continuously.

   a.   True   b.   False

18. The existence of noise traders injects imperfections into financial market and causes market values to diverge from economic values.

   a.   True   b.   False

19. The par value of a stock is not strongly correlated to its market price or economic value.

   a.   True   b.   False

20. For most companies the book value per share is a useful measure of the economic value of a share of stock.

   a.   True   b.   False

21. Liquidation value represents the cost of replacing assets on the firm's balance sheet at today's prices.

    a.   True   b.   False

22. The discounted dividend model implies that the value of a share of stock does not depend on the holding period of any particular investor.

    a.   True   b.   False

23. The Gordon model describes a stock's value as a function of its expected dividends, the market capitalization rate, and the expected growth rate in dividends.

    a.   True   b.   False

24. The discounted dividend model cannot be used for a stock that does not currently pay a dividend.

    a.   True   b.   False

25. The information content of dividends hypothesis states that managers signal their expectations about the firm's prospects through dividend policy.

    a.   True   b.   False

26. Economic earnings are easy to calculate from accounting earnings.

    a.   True   b.   False

27. The discounted cash flow model claims that dividend policy is irrelevant to the price of the firm's common stock.

    a.   True   b.   False

28. The price/earnings ratio is used as a yardstick to measure relative value.

    a.   True   b.   False

29. The empirical evidence indicates that unexpected changes in dividends are associated with insignificant changes in the stock price because the market is efficient.

    a.   True   b.   False

30. The empirical evidence indicates that when firms announce surprisingly good or bad earnings, investors take a long time to adjust the valuation of these stocks.

    a.   True   b.   False

31. The overreaction hypothesis suggests that investors should buy winner portfolios and sell loser portfolios.

    a.   True   b.   False

32. The variance bounds literature indicates that stock price volatility is too high to be attributed to discounted dividends.

    a.   True   b.   False

33. Similar to common shareholders, preferred stockholders have one vote for each preferred share owned.

    a.   True   b.   False

34. Most preferred stocks have cumulative dividends.

    a.   True   b.   False

35. The yield on a preferred stock of a given risk class is generally higher than that of a similar debt because the preferred stock is riskier.

    a.   True   b.   False

36. Which of the following is *true* of a preferred stock?

    a.   It is less risky than debt issued by the same company.
    b.   Its dividends are tax exempt for corporate holders.
    c.   Its dividends have higher priority than those of common stockholders.
    d.   Its dividends are always cumulative.
    e.   either c or d

37. According to the discounted dividend model

    a. the value of a stock is independent of the holding period of any investor.
    b. the value of a stock is a function of its expected dividends, the market capitalization rate, and the expected growth rate in dividends.
    c. the higher the discount rate, the lower the stock price.
    d. the capital structure of the firm is entirely equity.
    e. All of the above statements are correct.

38. Which of the following statements is *most* correct?

    a. The dividend rate of an adjustable-rate preferred stock is reset every 45 days in an auction process.
    b. Empirical studies find that unexpected changes in dividends are associated with changes in the stock price in the same direction.
    c. The discounted cash flow model developed by Modigliani and Miller states that the dividend policy is important in determining the price of a stock.
    d. In a perfectly efficient market, accounting earnings are equal to economic earnings.
    e. All of the above statements are correct.

SELF-TEST PROBLEMS

1. General Electric stock is currently traded on the NYSE at $90 per share. GE just paid an annual dividend of $2.52. You expect this dividend to grow at a constant rate of 7 percent. What is your market capitalization rate if you believe that $90 is a fair price for GE stock?

    a. 9.8 percent.
    b. 11 percent.
    c. 10 percent.
    d. 10.2 percent.
    e. none of the above

2. Chevron just paid a dividend of $3.50 per share. This dividend is expected to grow 10 percent for the next three years and 5 percent thereafter. The market capitalization rate for Chevron is 15 percent. According to the discounted dividend model, the fair price for Chevron stock is

   a. $58.52.
   b. $41.77.
   c. $37.58.
   d. $43.63.
   e. none of the above

(The following data apply to Self-Test Problems 3 through 6.)

The stock of Kellogg is selling at $52 per share. The company traditionally pays out 40 percent of its earnings in dividends and has enjoyed a consistent ROE of 20 percent. Earnings next year are expected to be $3 per share.

3. Assuming that the discounted dividend model accurately captures the stock's value, the rate of return investors expect to make when buying this stock at $52 is

   a. 14.31 percent.
   b. 20.00 percent.
   c. 15.46 percent.
   d. 10.31 percent.
   e. none of the above

4. If the retention rate is increased to 65 percent, the new Kellogg stock price is

   a. $52.00.
   b. $60.15.
   c. $34.80.
   d. $80.15.
   e. none of the above

5. Some of Kellogg's board members believe that increasing the dividend will have a positive effect on the stock's price. If the dividend payout is increased to 50 percent, the new Kellogg stock price is

   a. $52.00.
   b. $80.15.
   c. $36.80.
   d. $41.50.
   e. none of the above

6.   What action would you recommend to the board regarding dividends?

a.   The firm should increase dividends.
b.   The firm should maintain the current level of dividends.
c.   The firm should reduce dividends.
d.   The firm should declare a stock split and increase dividends.
e.   The firm should pay a stock dividend in addition to the current cash dividend.

ANSWERS TO SELF-TEST QUESTIONS

1.	economic	20.	False
2.	Noise	21.	False
3.	Book	22.	True
4.	Gordon	23.	True
5.	retention ratio	24.	False
6.	growth firm	25.	True
7.	accounting earnings	26.	False
8.	leading P/E	27.	True
9.	overreaction	28.	True
10.	speculative bubble	29.	False
11.	variance bounds	30.	True
12.	sinking fund	31.	False
13.	participating	32.	True
14.	conversion ratio	33.	False
15.	Dutch auction rate	34.	True
16.	True	35.	False
17.	False	36.	c
18.	True	37.	e
19.	True	38.	b

SOLUTIONS TO SELF-TEST PROBLEMS

1.   c.   Using the discounted dividend model, we have:

$$\$90 = [\$2.52(1.07)]/(k - 0.07)$$
$$k = \{2.52(1.07)]/90\} + 0.07 = 10\%$$

2.   b.   The present value of the dividends of Chevron in the next three years is:

Year	Dividend=$D_0(1+g)^t$	PV of dividend at 15% discount rate
0	$3.50	
1	$3.85	$3.35
2	$4.24	$3.21
3	$4.66	$3.06
		$9.62

Starting in year 4, the present value of all Chevron dividends, using the Gordon model, is:

$$[\$4.66(1.05)]/(0.15 - 0.05) = 4.89/0.10 = \$48.90$$

The present value of $48.90 at 15 percent discount rate is $32.15.
The fair price for Chevron stock is:
    $9.62 + 32.15 = $41.77.

3.   a.   The equation showing the rate of return that investors expect to make when buying Kellogg stock at $52 is:
    $$k = g + (D_1/P_0)$$

$P_0 = \$52,\ D_1 = 0.4(\$3) = \$1.20,\ g = 0.6(0.20) = 0.12$
    $k = 0.12 + (\$1.2/\$52) =\ 0.1431$

4.   d.   If $b = 0.65$, then $g = 0.65(0.20) = 0.13$
and $D_1 = 0.35(\$3) = \$1.05$
The new Kellogg stock price is:
$P_0 = \$1.05/(0.1431 - 0.13) = \$80.15$

5.   e. $D_1 = 0.5(\$3) = \$1.5,\ \ g = (0.5)(0.2) = 0.10$
When the dividend payout rate is 50 percent, the Kellogg stock price is:
$P_0 = \$1.50/(0.1431 - 0.10) = \$34.80$

6.   c.   Because Kellogg can earn more (20 percent) than the market required rate of 14.31%, the company should reduce dividends.

CHAPTER 16

FUNDAMENTAL AND TECHNICAL ANALYSIS

OVERVIEW

This chapter illustrates the following: (1) fundamental analysis; (2) ways in which reported earnings per share can be affected by accounting procedures for depreciation, inventory, and acquisitions; (3) how ratio analysis can be used to evaluate the fundamental financial health of the company; (4) how to calculate and analyze the growth rate of a company; (5) technical analysis; and (6) the implications of the efficient-market hypothesis for fundamental and technical analysis.

OUTLINE

I. Fundamental analysis focuses on the accounting and economic factors about a company that should determine the true worth of its stock.

   A. Accounting earnings—In order to do fundamental analysis, we must predict future earnings and growth in earnings. Because companies do not report economic earnings, analysts must use accounting earnings reported on financial statements. Most companies keep two sets of books, one for financial reporting and the other for tax purposes.

   B. How accounting procedures affect reported earnings and cash flow:

      1. Accounting for inventory FIFO versus LIFO—The procedure chosen to value inventory affects the reported cost of goods sold on the income statement and the inventory on the balance sheet. Differences will result in the income reported between FIFO (first-in-first-out) and LIFO (last-in-first-out) if the prices paid for the inventory change during the year. Studies conducted on firms that switch from FIFO to LIFO find that the firm's share price increases 5 percent on average, closely reflecting the discounted tax savings from the switch.

      2. Depreciation expense—Most firms use accelerated depreciation methods for tax reporting and straight-line depreciation for financial reporting. Different firms can use different depreciation methods, making comparability among firms difficult.

      3. Accounting for acquisitions: purchase versus pooling—Under the purchase method, the premium paid over the fair value of the seller's assets is

167

recorded as goodwill, which is then amortized against earnings on an after-tax basis. Under the pooling method, the book value of the acquired firm's assets is added to the book value of the buyer's assets and all affected accounts on the balance sheet are adjusted.

4. Expending versus capitalizing expenditures—Most firms generally prefer to expense all purchases because it reduces current taxable income and lowers their tax liability. However, this procedure reduces reported income, lowers the book value of the firm and inflates future earnings.

5. Adjusting for discontinued operations and extraordinary items—Because of the non-recurring nature of extraordinary items, the fundamental analyst faces a dilemma in determining how these items should be used to calculate economic earnings.

C. Analyzing the quality of reported earnings—In addition to estimating the economic earnings of a company, the analyst must examine its financial statements to evaluate the quality of earnings. Quality refers to how the company generates its return on equity and its ability to maintain or increase its rate of return in the future. Higher marks will be given to firms whose earnings are derived from profits of primary business operations and asset management rather than from excessive use of debt or aggressive accounting procedures.

D. Financial ratio analysis.

1. Rate of return on equity (ROE)—Is net profit divided by common equity. The ROE is a product of net profit margin, total asset turnover, and the equity multiplier.

$$ROE = \frac{Net\ profit}{Sales} \times \frac{Sales}{Total\ assets} \times \frac{Total\ assets}{Common\ equity} \qquad (16.1)$$

2. Liquidity ratios measure a company's ability to pay short-term obligations. The two most common liquidity ratios are the current ratio and the quick ratio. The current ratio is current assets divided by current liabilities. The quick ratio is calculated as [(Current assets–Inventory)/(Current liabilities)].

3. Turnover ratios measure the utilization of different types of assets. Common measures are inventory turnover, accounts receivable collection period, fixed-asset turnover, and total asset turnover.

4. Financial structure ratios measure the extent that debt is used in the firm's financial structure. Common measures are debt-to-total-assets ratio, times-interest-earned ratio, and the equity multiplier.

E. Can fundamental analysis predict future stock price performance? Empirical evidence indicates that portfolio managers who use fundamental analysis for stock selection are unable to outperform the market. The large number of analysts who continually monitor and evaluate companies make the stock market efficient. As analysts discover new information about a company, that information is quickly impounded into the stock price. Thus, it is difficult to earn an above-average return.

F. Value Line: The case for fundamental analysis—Value Line Investment Survey is a rich source of fundamental security data. Each week Value Line ranks common stocks from 1 (best) to 5 (worst) based primarily on past and projected earnings and on other financial statement variables in its data base. There is some evidence that Value Line recommendations, especially changes in rankings, can be used to outperform the market.

II. Technical analysis is based on the premise that all information about a stock is reflected in the past sequence of its prices. As new information flows to the market, stock prices tend to form patterns, allowing future prices to be predicted because these patterns repeat themselves over time.

A. Why technical analysis is supposed to work? Reasons given for the use of technical analysis include: (1) price is affected by supply and demand, (2) prices move in trends that persist, (3) changes in trends are affected by changes in supply and demand, (4) trends repeat themselves over time, and (5) supply and demand are influenced by rational and irrational factors.

B. Analysis of stock prices.

1. Trends in a stock price are the primary pattern that the technician tries to determine. The trend can be upward, downward, or neutral, in which a stock builds a base to appreciate in the future.
2. Divergence shows the relation between one top (bottom) and the subsequent top (bottom). A bearish divergence occurs when subsequent tops are lower than the previous one.
3. Popular patterns include head and shoulders, pennant, wedge, channels, saucer, and so on.
4. Moving averages are calculated by summing the most recent n days of prices and dividing by n. The purpose of the moving average is to smooth the data and eliminate extreme stock prices. A buy signal is given when the daily stock price rises through the moving average line, and a sale signal occurs when the price falls below the moving-average line.
5. Relative strength index is calculated by dividing the number of "up" closes by the sum of "up" and "down" closes in the period and multiplying the result by 100. When the ratio goes above 70, the market has reached a top, and a sell signal is given. If the ratio falls below 30, it is time to buy because the market will reverse itself.

169

6. Momentum is designed to tell if prices are changing at an increasing or a decreasing rate. The momentum in a period is the momentum in the previous period plus the change in price in that period. The daily momentum values are plotted on a graph relative to a zero line. The rule is to buy when the indicator crosses up through the zero line from underneath, and to sell when it falls below the zero line from above.

7. A support level is a narrow price range at which an increase is expected in the demand for a stock, thus providing a floor on the price. A resistance level is a narrow price range at which the technician expects additional supply of the stock, thus providing a ceiling for price increase.

8. A stock that is overbought is too high relative to where it will be in the near future and thus is predicted to fall in price. A stock that is oversold has been driven too low and should recover in the near future.

9. Accumulation-distribution is used to find divergence, that is the turning point in a trend. It consists of a cumulative index that adds or subtracts portions of daily price changes over an arbitrary time period.

10. To apply the filter rule, first the technician selects a filter that is a percentage of the stock price. If the stock goes up by the filter or more, buy and hold the stock until it goes down by at least the filter from the high, then liquidate the stock and sell short. The goal of the filter rule is to get on a trend when the trend is starting and to get out as it begins to change.

B. Other technical indicators.

1. Mutual fund cash positions—The cash balances of mutual funds are used by technicians as a contrary indicator. When the cash balances rise to an abnormally high level, technicians become bullish on the market and vice versa when cash balances become too low.

2. Put/Call ratio represents the ratio of put option contracts to call option contracts that are outstanding. The ratio tends to fluctuate between 0.65 and 0.30. If it moves above 0.65, the contrary technician would buy. If the ratio falls below 0.40, the technician would sell.

3. Opinions of investment advisory services are a contrary indicator which claims that a bearish signal occurs when the percentage of advisors who are bullish on the market surpasses 60 percent of all services rendering an opinion. A bullish signal occurs when the percentage falls below 20 percent of the total recommendations.

C. Can technical analysis predict the future? Because technical analysis is as much an art as a science, it is impossible to prove that the approach does or does not work. The overwhelming empirical evidence indicates that different types of technical indicates do not provide information about the future prices of securities that would allow the users to outperform the market, especially when transaction costs are considered.

III. Fundamental technical analysis and market efficiency—The objective of fundamental analysis is to determine the true value of a stock by analyzing all the available information about the company. Given that thousands of analysts are carefully examining information about companies, any new information is rapidly reflected in the stock price. The technical analyst tries to predict the future price from a series of past prices. Technical analysis would be logical if stock prices follow trends and if information is disseminated gradually to market participants. But that does not appear to be the case. Therefore, picking stocks on the basis of fundamental or technical analysis will not result in superior performance in an efficient market.

VOCABULARY REVIEW

fundamental analysis
technical analysis
FIFO (first-in first-out)
LIFO (last-in first-out)
accelerated depreciation
pooling method
net profit margin
equity multiplier
financial leverage
current ratio
quick ratio
inventory turnover
net working capital
accounts receivable
   collection period
times-interest-earned ratio

market value to book value ratio
bar chart
contrary indicator
trend
bear trap
divergence
head and shoulders
moving average
relative-strength index
momentum
support and resistance levels
overbought and oversold
accumulation-distribution
filter rule
put/call ratio

SELF-TEST QUESTIONS

Definitional

1. _____ _____ focuses on accounting data and economic factors to estimate the intrinsic value of a stock.

2. An approach to predict the future stock price over a very short horizon by detecting trends in a series of past stock prices is called _____ _____.

3.	The _____ inventory valuation method assumes that the most recently purchased inventory is sold first and any remaining inventory carried forward will consist of the oldest inventory.

4.	The accounting method for acquisitions which assumes that the premium paid over the fair value of the seller's assets is recorded in a goodwill account is called the _____ method.

5.	The ratio of total assets over common equity is called the _____ _____ _____ .

6.	_____ _____ _____ represents the difference between current assets and current liabilities.

7.	The ratio of earnings before interest and taxes over the interest expense is called the _____ - _____ - _____ ratio.

8.	A _____ _____ consists of a vertical bar with its top at the security's high for the day and its bottom at its daily low, with a hatch mark indicating the closing price in a trend.

9.	A bearish _____ occurs in a trend when a security's subsequent top is lower than the previous one.

10.	The 150 day _____ _____ is calculated by summing the most recent 150 days of stock prices and dividing by 150.

11.	The _____ indicator is designed to tell if prices are changing at an increasing or a decreasing rate.

12.	A narrow price range at which technicians expect an increase in the demand for a stock, thus providing a floor on prices is called the _____ _____ .

13.	Technicians claim that a stock which is _____ has been driven down to low and should recover in the near future.

Conceptual

14.	Most security analysts are technical analysts.

	a.	True			b.	False

15. It is legal for firms to keep two sets of books, one for financial reporting and the other for tax purposes.

    a.   True   b.   False

16. When firms report financial statements to shareholders, the objective is to make reported earnings as small as possible to produce the smallest tax liability.

    a.   True   b.   False

17. The FIFO method minimizes the firm's tax liability and increases its cash flow.

    a.   True   b.   False

18. Because security analysts can easily adjust accounting earnings for tax-driven manipulations, firms that switch from FIFO to LIFO do not experience a significant increase in stock price.

    a.   True   b.   False

19. The method used to depreciate assets can have a dramatic effect on the reported earnings of a company.

    a.   True   b.   False

20. A firm can use different inventory valuation methods for tax and financial reporting.

    a.   True   b.   False

21. In a high inflationary period, all acceptable depreciation methods will understate the replacement cost of the asset and thus overstate income.

    a.   True   b.   False

22. Under the purchase method for acquisitions, the book value of the acquired firm's assets is added to the book value of the buyer's assets and all affected accounts on the balance sheet are adjusted.

    a.   True   b.   False

23. The rate of return on equity is not directly affected by the total asset turnover.

    a.   True   b.   False

24. Leverage will work to magnify the rate of return on equity to the positive side in good times, but it does not magnify ROE on the downside.

    a.   True   b.   False

25. The quick ratio can never be larger than the current ratio.

    a.   True   b.   False

26. A poor accounts receivable collection period will have an adverse effect on the total asset turnover ratio.

    a.   True   b.   False

27. Most empirical studies indicate that strategies based on fundamental analysis do not generate abnormal returns.

    a.   True   b.   False

28. Technical analysis is consistent with the efficient market hypothesis.

    a.   True   b.   False

29. Technicians believe that future stock prices can be predicted over a long time horizon by detecting trends in a series of past stock prices.

    a.   True   b.   False

30. Technical analysis assumes that prices tend to move in trends, and new information is reflected in stock prices quickly.

    a.   True   b.   False

31. It is possible that two technicians may come up with different interpretations and patterns from the same price chart.

    a.   True   b.   False

32. Technicians claim that a sell signal occurs when the stock price falls by at least the filter percentage from the previous high.

    a.   True   b.   False

33. The put/call ratio is a contrary indicator of technical analysis.

  a.   True   b.   False

34. If the market is efficient, neither fundamental analysis nor technical analysis can generate abnormal returns.

  a.   True   b.   False

35. Which of the following is *true* for technical analysis?

  a.   It assumes that prices tend to move in trends that persist for an appreciable time.
  b.   It assumes that new information is quickly disseminated in stock prices.
  c.   It assumes that the patterns or trends tend to repeat themselves over time.
  d.   It is consistent with the weak-form of the efficient market hypothesis.
  e.   both a and c.

36. According to fundamental analysis,

  a.   an analyst should give a buy recommendation when the market value of the stock is higher than the intrinsic value.
  b.   all information about a stock is reflected in the past sequence of its prices.
  c.   comparability among firms can be accomplished by adjusting accounting earnings for different accounting rules that can be used.
  d.   accounting and economic earnings are the same.
  e.   stock prices tend to move in trends.

37. Which of the following is *not* a technical indicator?

  a.   filter rule
  b.   divergence
  c.   put/call ratio
  d.   Gordon model
  e.   all of the above

38. Which of the following is associated with fundamental analysis?

  a.   trading volume
  b.   P/E ratio
  c.   momentum
  d.   moving average
  e.   all of the above

SELF-TEST PROBLEMS

(The following data apply to self-test problems 1 through 3.)

Service Corporation International reports the following information in its annual report (in millions):

	1991	1992
Total assets	$2,123	$2,611
Net sale	643	772
Net income	73	87
Income taxes	36	53
Interest expense	54	42
Common equity	615	683
Common shares outstanding (thousands)	71,426	76,856

1.   The earnings per share for 1991 and 1992 are

   a. $0.95 and $1.14.
   b. $1.02 and $1.13.
   c. $1.53 and $1.82.
   d. $1.07 and $1.00.
   e.   none of the above

2.   The times-interest-earned ratio and the rate of return on equity for 1992 are

   a.   4.33 and 12.74 percent.
   b.   3.01 and 11.87 percent.
   c.   4.33 and 11.87 percent.
   d.   3.33 and 12.74 percent.
   e.   none of the above

3.   The equity multiplier and the book value per share for 1991 are

   a.   3.82 and $8.89.
   b.   3.82 and $8.61.
   c.   3.45 and $8.89.
   d.   3.45 and $8.61.
   e.   none of the above

(The following data apply to Self-Test Problems 4 through 7.)

Consider the following data (in millions of dollars except per share data) for Sprint and MCI:

	Sprint	MCI
Net sales	$4,513.20	$5,810.50
Net profit	429.50	591.70
Total assets	5,871.30	6,091.70
Common Equity	2,953.20	3,101.20
Dividends per share	0.00	1.52
Earnings per share	3.10	3.70

4.   The net profit margins for Sprint and MCI are

   a.   9.52 percent and 9.81 percent.
   b.   10.40 percent and 11.52 percent.
   c.   9.52 percent and 10.18 percent.
   d.   8.59 percent and 10.47 percent.
   e.   none of the above

5.   The equity multipliers for Sprint and MCI are

   a.   1.9881 and 1.8710.
   b.   2.1210 and 1.9643.
   c.   1.9881 and 1.9643.
   d.   1.8052 and 1.7514.
   e.   none of the above

6.   The ROEs for Sprint and MCI are

   a.   16.20 percent and 20.14 percent.
   b.   14.54 percent and 19.08 percent.
   c.   15.21 percent and 19.08 percent.
   d.   14.54 percent and 11.24 percent.
   e.   none of the above

7.   The expected growth in earnings for Sprint and MCI are

   a.   14.54 percent and 10.24 percent.
   b.   13.90 percent and 11.24 percent.
   c.   16.22 percent and 13.10 percent.
   d.   15.61 percent and 11.24 percent.
   e.   none of the above

ANSWERS TO SELF-TEST QUESTIONS

1.	Fundamental analysis		20.	False
2.	technical analysis		21.	True
3.	LIFO		22.	False
4.	purchase		23.	False
5.	equity multiplier		24.	False
6.	Net working capital		25.	True
7.	times-interest-earned		26.	True
8.	bar chart		27.	True
9.	divergence		28.	False
10.	moving average		29.	False
11.	momentum		30.	False
12.	support level		31.	True
13.	oversold		32.	True
14.	False		33.	True
15.	True		34.	True
16.	False		35.	e
17.	False		36.	c
18.	False		37.	d
19.	True		38.	b

SOLUTIONS TO SELF-TEST PROBLEMS

1. b. The earnings per share for 1991 are:
(Net income)/(Common shares outstanding)
For 1991, $73/71.426 = $1.02
For 1992, $87/76.856 = $1.13

2. a. The times-interest-earned ratio for 1992 is:
(Earnings before interest and taxes)/(interest expense)
($87 + $42 + $53)/$42 = 4.33
The rate of return on equity for 1992 is:
(Net income)/(Common equity)
$87/$683 = 12.74%

3. d. The equity multiplier for 1991 is:
(Total assets)/(Common equity)
$2,123/$615 = 3.45
The book value per share for 1991 is:
$615/71.426 = $8.61

4.   c.   The net profit margin of Sprint is:
$429.50/$4,513.20 = 9.52%

The net profit margin of MCI is:
$591.70/$5,810.50 = 10.18%

5.   c.   The equity multiplier of Sprint is:
$5,871.30/$2,953.20 = 1.9881

The equity multiplier of MCI is:
$6,091.70/$3,101.20 = 1.9643

6.   b.   The ROE of Sprint is:
$429.50/$2,953.20 = 14.54%

The ROE of MCI is:
$591.70/$3,101.20 = 19.08%

7.   e.   The expected growth in earnings for Sprint is:

$$g = \text{retention ratio x ROE}$$
$$= [(\$3.10-0)/\$3.1] \times 14.54\% = 14.54\%$$

The expected growth in earnings for MCI is:

$$g = [(\$3.70-\$1.52)/\$3.70] \times 19.08\% = 11.24\%$$

CHAPTER 17

INSTITUTIONAL INVESTORS AND PORTFOLIO

MANAGEMENT IN PRACTICE

OVERVIEW

This chapter illustrates the following: (1) implications of the efficient-market hypothesis for portfolio management, (2) types and characteristics of mutual funds, (3) defined-benefit and defined-contribution pension plans, (4) functions performed by bank trust departments and trust companies in institutional investment management, (5) investment objectives of life and casualty insurance companies, (6) passive and active portfolio management styles, (7) how active managers use market timing, management styles, and factor models to construct portfolios, and (8) results of studies that examine the benefits and disadvantages of trying to time the market.

OUTLINE

I.   Portfolio management and the efficient market hypothesis—If the market is semistrong-form efficient, investors should buy and hold a broadly diversified portfolios, adjusting for risk by allocating funds between the risky market portfolio and Treasury securities. The appropriate risk/expected-return tradeoff is determined by the investor's utility function. Transaction and search costs should be minimized.

II.   Mutual funds.

      A.   Closed-end funds issue shares through an initial public offering. Once all the shares are sold, the offering is closed. The investment company neither redeems its shares nor issues new shares. The fund shares are traded in the secondary market such as the NYSE. Typically, closed-end fund shares sell at a discount below the net asset value (NAV) per share. Empirical evidence indicates that buying closed-end fund shares at a discount from NAV results in abnormal returns.

      B.   Open-end funds sell shares to any individual wishing to own them and stand ready to redeem shares which individuals want to sell. All transactions occur directly between the fund and the investor, not in a secondary market.

C.   The net asset value:

$$NAV = \frac{\begin{array}{c}Market\ value\\of\ fund\ assets\end{array} - \begin{array}{c}Outstanding\\liabilities\end{array}}{Number\ of\ shares\ outstanding}$$ (17.1)

D.   Fees charged by mutual funds—Many open-end funds charge a front-end load when investors buy shares of the fund. Some funds also charge a back-end load or redemption fee when shareholders sell shares back to the fund. All funds levy annual management fees. In addition, over one-half of all open-end funds charge a 12b-1 fee to cover sales commissions and advertising costs.

E.   Mutual fund benefits are professional investment management, diversification, attractive shareholder services, and possible superior performance.

F.   Studies of mutual fund performance indicate that mutual fund managers do not possess superior information that would allow them to outperform the market, especially after all costs are considered.

III.   Pension funds receive contributions from a company and its employees and invest the money to fund payments to employees when they retire.

A.   A defined-contribution plan specifies the amount each employee and the company must contribute to the pension fund each year. No commitment is made regarding the employee's benefit upon retirement. The employees bear the market risk but reap the reward of higher-than-expected earnings.

B.   A defined-benefit plan specifies the yearly retirement benefit that each employee will receive, but it sets no requirement on the yearly contributions that must be made. The company bears the market risk but shares in the benefits of good investment performance. If the pension fund is underfunded because the present value of the fund's liabilities exceeds its assets, this obligation must be reported on the company's balance sheet.

IV.   Bank trust departments and trust companies provide professional investment management of trust assets for their customers. A trust enables the grantor to control how his wealth is managed after he dies. A trust is created in which a trustee is designated to manage the assets for the beneficiary. Trusts are important as a means by which to reduce the amount of estate taxes that the heirs must pay.

V.   Endowment funds represent contributions to educational institutions, religious organizations, and other nonprofit organizations. Most institutions use outside money managers to invest their funds. Endowments do not have a contractual obligation that must be met or shareholders who must be satisfied. Instead, they have to balance the organization's need for current income with the requirement that the endowment grow over time to meet future needs.

VI. Insurance companies.

    A.   Life insurance companies have highly predictable cash outflows (death payments) and inflows (premiums received). Their investment horizon is long term, typically over 30 years, to match the company's liabilities, and the liquidity needs are low.

    B.   Casualty insurance companies have high variability in cash flows because casualty claims can be large and unpredictable. Therefore, liquidity in the investment portfolio is important. Most casualty companies concentrate on bond and stock investments to satisfy the liquidity needs and long-term capital appreciation.

VII. Institutional management of portfolios.

    A.   Passive portfolio management—Managers try to replicate some target portfolio using full replication, a sampling approach of buying a subset of the target portfolio, or partial replication in which a smaller portfolio of stocks is selected and weighted according to industries represented in the target index.

    B.   Active portfolio management—Most active strategies generate significant trading costs.

        1.   Market timing is the strategy of changing the fund's allocation among stocks, bonds, and money market securities over time in an effort to capture gains in bull markets and avoid losses in bear markets.

        2.   Management styles—Using a top-down approach, the manager emphasizes particular sectors or industries that are expected to outperform the market. The manager proceeds from macro forecasts about the economy, then to forecasts about the sectors, and finally to analyses of particular stocks in those sectors. With the bottom-up approach, the manager picks individual stocks that are undervalued and expected to outperform the market. Macro forecasts and market themes are not important.

        3.   Factor models use regression equations to identify important factors and then select stocks that benefit from a change in those factors.

VOCABULARY REVIEW

indexing
open-end fund
closed-end fund
mutual fund
net asset value
load fee
back-end load
12b-1 fee
personal agency account
full replication
partial replication
completeness fund
tactical asset allocation
growth manager
bottom-up management style

defined-contribution plan
defined-benefit plan
trust company
grantor
beneficiary
personal trust account
pension fund
common trust account
endowment fund
sampling approach
quadratic optimization program
market timing
value manager
top-down management style
factor model

SELF-TEST QUESTIONS

Definitional

1. An investment fund which neither redeems shares nor issues additional shares is called a _____ _____ fund.

2. The fee charged by mutual funds to cover advertising costs and sales commissions is called the _____ _____.

3. A _____ _____ represents a commission charged by a mutual fund when an investor buys its shares.

4. The _____ _____ plan specifies the yearly retirement benefit that each employee will receive, but it sets no requirement on the yearly contributions that must be made.

5. The target portfolio to which a fund manager's performance is compared with is called a _____ _____.

6. For a _____ _____ account, the trustee does not take title to the trust assets but simply buys and sells portfolio assets as an agent of the owner.

7. Strategies that attempt to add value by profiting from forecasted market movements are called _____ portfolio management strategies.

8.   The difference between the managed passive portfolio and the index it tries to replicate is termed _____ _____.

9.   The strategy of changing the fund's allocation among stocks, bonds, and Treasury securities over time in an effort to capture gains in bull markets and avoid losses in bear markets is called _____ _____.

10.   The _____ _____ approach is a management style that starts from macro forecasts about the economy, then to forecasts about an industry, and finally to analysis of a company.

Conceptual

11.   The efficient market hypothesis is completely accepted by all professional investors.

        a.   True   b.   False

12.   Indexing means to buy and hold a broadly diversified portfolio of stocks that mimics an index such as the S&P 500.

        a.   True   b.   False

13.   The growth fund type is the most popular category of stock mutual funds.

        a.   True   b.   False

14.   Closed-end funds typically sell at a premium over their net asset value per share.

        a.   True   b.   False

15.   Because closed-end funds continually buy and sell new shares, their cash balance available for investment can fluctuate a lot.

        a.   True   b.   False

16.   Only open-end funds levy annual management fees.

        a.   True   b.   False

17.   All closed-end and open-end funds charge a 12b-1 fee to pay for advertising costs.

        a.   True   b.   False

18. Empirical evidence indicates that in the past mutual funds have not, on average, outperformed an unmanaged index portfolio.

    a.   True   b.   False

19. Private-company and public-employee pension funds represent a very small segment of professionally managed portfolios.

    a.   True   b.   False

20. Most pension funds are structured as defined-contribution plans.

    a.   True   b.   False

21. Under a defined-benefit plan, the company bears the market risk and must increase its contribution to the plan if the investment performance is inadequate.

    a.   True   b.   False

22. Trusts are an important vehicle to control the amount of estate taxes that must be paid upon death.

    a.   True   b.   False

23. Most nonprofit organizations use internal managers to invest their endowment funds.

    a.   True   b.   False

24. Life insurance companies have much lower liquidity needs than casualty insurance companies.

    a.   True   b.   False

25. Market timing and the use of factor models to select stocks are two general approaches to active portfolio management.

    a.   True   b.   False

26. Value managers focus on a narrow market niche such as small-capitalization firms.

    a.   True   b.   False

27. Which of the following is *not* an example of passive portfolio management?

    a.   partial replication
    b.   sampling approach
    c.   bottom-up management style
    d.   full replication
    e.   All of the above are examples of passive portfolio management.

28. Which of the following statements is *most* correct?

    a.   Open-end fund shares can be traded above or below the net asset value per share, depending on the demand and supply of the shares.
    b.   All mutual funds charge a load fee to cover sales expenses.
    c.   Tactical asset allocation is an active portfolio management strategy.
    d.   Only very wealthy people should use trusts.
    e.   Factor models to identify stocks are used primarily by passive portfolio managers.

29. Which of the following is *not* a benefit of investing in mutual funds?

    a.   professional investment management
    b.   performance superior to the market portfolio
    c.   instant diversification
    d.   attractive shareholder services
    e.   all of the above

SELF-TEST PROBLEMS

(The following data apply to Self-Test Problems 1 through 3.)

The Windsor mutual fund has an investment portfolio with a market value of $958 million. The fund has outstanding liabilities of $2.1 million.

1. If the Windsor fund has 22 million shares outstanding, the net asset value today is

    a. $43.55.
    b. $43.45.
    c. $42.90.
    d. $43.71.
    e.   none of the above

2. On the following day the fund's assets increase in value to $969 million, while the liabilities and outstanding shares remain the same. The new net asset value of Windsor fund is

a. $44.05.
b. $44.01.
c. $43.95.
d. $43.45.
e.   none of the above

3. The one-day rate of return of the Windsor fund is

a.   1.15 percent.
b.   1.21 percent.
c.   2.01 percent.
d.   1.04 percent.
e.   none of the above

ANSWERS TO SELF-TEST QUESTIONS

1.	closed-end		16.	False
2.	12b-1 fee		17.	False
3.	load fee		18.	True
4.	defined-benefit		19.	False
5.	benchmark portfolio		20.	False
6.	personal agency		21.	True
7.	active		22.	True
8.	tracking error		23.	False
9.	market timing		24.	True
10.	top-down		25.	True
11.	False		26.	False
12.	True		27.	c
13.	True		28.	c
14.	False		29.	b
15.	False			

SOLUTIONS TO SELF-TEST PROBLEMS

1.   b.   The net asset value of the Windsor fund is:
            NAV = (Assets − Liabilities)/Number of Shares
                = ($958 million − $2.1 million)/22 million
                = $43.45

2.   c.   The new net asset value of the Windsor fund is:

$$\text{NAV} = (\$969 \text{ million} - \$2.1 \text{ million})/22 \text{ million}$$
$$= \$43.95$$

3.   a.   The one-day rate of return of the Windsor fund is:

$$(\$43.95 - \$43.45)/\$43.45 = 1.15\%$$

CHAPTER 18

CHARACTERISTICS AND VALUATION OF PUT

AND CALL OPTIONS

OVERVIEW

This chapter describes the terms and characteristics of put and call options and gives you a better understanding of the following: (1) the roles of the Option Clearing Corporation and the option market participants in option trading, (2) profit and loss diagrams for simple option positions, (3) the creation of a synthetic option on a stock, (4) the Black-Scholes model to value call and put options; and (5) other securities which have option-like characteristics.

OUTLINE

I. Terminology and characteristics of options.

   A. A call (put) is a contract giving the buyer the right, but not the obligation, to buy (sell) the underlying asset, such as 100 shares of a particular stock, at a fixed exercise price on or before the expiration date. The seller is called the option writer. The number of contracts outstanding is called open interest. When a call's exercise price is above the current stock price, the call is out-of-the-money. A call whose exercise price is below the stock price is called in-the-money. The Options Clearing Corporation (OCC) performs the clearing function for all listed options, meaning that they match and settle all outstanding contracts at option expiration. Most options expire on the Saturday following the third Friday of the option's expiration month. The difference between the stock price and the option's exercise price is called the intrinsic value.

II. The marketplace for options.

   A. Option exchanges—The two largest option exchanges are the Chicago Board Option Exchange (CBOE) and the American Stock Exchange (AMEX). To make secondary trading possible, the option exchanges establish two things: (1) standardized terms in exercise price, expiration date, and contract size; and (2) the Option Clearing Corporation, which becomes the buyer for every option seller and the seller for every option buyer, thus guaranteeing performance on each contract.

B.   In addition to options on individual stocks, other underlying assets which have options available are:

1.   Options on stock indexes—Popular index options include those on the S&P 100 Index, S&P 500 Index, and major market index. Index options are settled in cash rather than by delivery of the underlying asset.
2.   Interest rate options—Options on Treasury bonds and bills are available, but the volume of trading is low.
3.   Options on foreign currency—These options specify delivery of a fixed amount of foreign currency upon exercise.
4.   Options on futures—Options on futures are options whose underlying asset is a futures contract rather than the asset itself.
5.   Long term equity options—These options are identical to individual equity options except that their maturity date is up to two years in the future.
6.   International stock index warrants—They are essentially long term options on an index of foreign stocks. Most index warrants trade on the AMEX and have an expiration date two to five years from time of issuance.

III.   Profit and loss at option maturity.

A.   Buying and selling a call—Buying a call offers limited downside exposure with unlimited upside potential. Thus, the call has an insurance feature compared to ownership of the stock. The call writer is a seller of insurance.

B.   Buying and selling a put—A put buyer profits if the stock price falls, but is protected if the stock price appreciates because he cannot lose more than the put premium.

IV.   Valuing an option prior to expiration—Options typically sell for an amount greater than the intrinsic value. The premium above the intrinsic value is called the time value of the option.

A.   The binomial pricing model assumes that the stock price follows a binomial process, meaning that it can only take one of two values at the end of any defined period. By working backward through each path of the price tree, the value of an option is found.

B.   The Black-Scholes option pricing model—The five input variables needed to calculate the Black-Scholes price are: the stock price, the exercise price, the time to maturity, the riskless rate of interest, and the stock's volatility. The formula's value is very sensitive to the estimate of volatility. The Black-Scholes model can be used to price European call or put options on stocks that will pay no dividends.

option position. Delta is the change in the call price with respect to a change in the price of the stock.

$$C = N(d_1)S - E(e^{-rt})N(d_2) \tag{18.5}$$

$$d_1 = \frac{\ln(\frac{S}{E}) + (r + \frac{\sigma^2}{2})T}{\sigma\sqrt{T}}$$

$$d_2 = d_1 - \sigma\sqrt{T}$$

where

C	=	call price
S	=	stock price
E	=	exercise price of the option
r	=	riskless rate of interest
σ	=	standard deviation of the stock's return
T	=	time of expiration of the option
e	=	base of the natural logarithms
$\ln(S/E)$	=	natural log of S/E
$N(d)$	=	value of the cumulative normal distribution evaluated at d_1 and d_2.

The Black-Scholes put-pricing model equation is:

$$P = -N(-d_1)S + E(e^{-rT})N(-d_2) \tag{18.6}$$

V.   Securities with option-like features.

A.   Callable bonds: give the issuer the right to redeem the bond before maturity at a specified price. Thus, the company can be viewed as holding a call option on the bond.

B.   Warrants are certificates which give the holder the right to purchase a specified number of common shares for a specified price on or before maturity. Warrant maturities are longer than listed options, ranging from two to ten years. When warrants are exercised, the number of shares outstanding is increased and the issuing firm receives cash equal to the exercise price.

C.   Convertible bonds can be exchanged by the holder for a specified number of shares of the issuer's common stock. Because a convertible bond can be thought of as a straight bond plus a warrant, it can be valued by calculating the worth of each component and summing them.

VOCABULARY REVIEW

American Option	insurance feature
European Option	time value
call	derivative security
put	binomial model
option writer	Black-Scholes model
intrinsic value	implied volatility
Option Clearing Corporation	delta
warrant	hedge ratio
open interest	covered call
strike price	dilution effect
out-of-the-money option	conversion ratio
in-the-money option	conversion parity price

SELF-TEST QUESTIONS

Definitional

1. A _____ is a contract giving the buyer of the option the right, but not the obligation, to sell the stock.

2. A _____ option can be exercised only on the expiration date.

3. The number of contracts outstanding at any point in time is called _____ _____.

4. When the strike price is below the current stock price, the call is _____ _____ _____.

5. _____ _____ is the difference between the value of the underlying asset and the option's exercise price.

6. Options on the Standard and Poor's 100 Index are examples of _____ _____.

7. The option premium above the intrinsic value is called the _____ _____.

8. Options are called _____ _____ because their value is derived from the value of their underlying security.

9.   The _____ model assumes that the stock price can take on only one of two values at the end of any defined period.

10.   The _____ is the change in the call price for a given change in stock price.

11.   A _____ _____ gives the issuing company the right to redeem the bond before maturity at a specified price.

12.   A _____ is a certificate which gives the holder the right to purchase a specified number of common shares at the exercise price on or before maturity.

13.   The number of common shares the convertible bondholder will receive upon conversion is called the _____ _____.

Conceptual

14.   Options which give the holder the right to conduct a transaction at a future date have existed since 1973.

      a.   True   b.   False

15.   A put decreases in value when the stock price falls and increases in value when the stock rises in price.

      a.   True   b.   False

16.   A call option is out-of-the-money when its exercise price is above the stock price.

      a.   True   b.   False

17.   The intrinsic value of a call or a put cannot be less than zero.

      a.   True   b.   False

18.   In order to list options on a stock, the option exchange must get the approval from the management of the company.

      a.   True   b.   False

19.   The Options Clearing Corporation delinks individual option buyers and sellers, thus allowing each party to trade independently in a secondary market.

      a.   True   b.   False

20. The exercise prices of options on stocks selling for less than $25 per share are set at $5 increments.

   a.   True   b.   False

21. Both individual stock options and index options are settled by delivery of the underlying asset.

   a.   True   b.   False

22. Foreign currency options expire on the Saturday following the third Friday of the month.

   a.   True   b.   False

23. Long term equity options have a maturity up to two years in the future.

   a.   True   b.   False

24. The buyer of a call option has limited downside exposure with unlimited upside potential.

   a.   True   b.   False

25. The binomial pricing model provides an analytical solution to the option price which can be determined from a formula.

   a.   True   b.   False

26. The most important variable in the Black-Scholes model is the stock price.

   a.   True   b.   False

27. A call should never be exercised before maturity if the stock does not pay a dividend.

   a.   True   b.   False

28. The delta for a call equals $N(d_1)$, and is referred to as the hedge ratio.

   a.   True   b.   False

29. The Black-Scholes model cannot be used to price European puts.

   a.   True   b.   False

30. A put should never be exercised before maturity when the stock pays no dividend.

a. True   b. False

31. Warrant maturities are typically much longer than listed options.

a. True   b. False

32. Exercising a warrant or a call will dilute the value of all shares.

a. True   b. False

33. A convertible bond can be thought of as a straight bond plus a warrant.

a. True   b. False

34. Which of the following statements is *most* correct?

a. The exercise price of an option is fully adjusted for a payment of cash dividend.
b. European options can be exercised on or before the expiration date.
c. Listed options 'on individual stocks expire on the Saturday following the third Friday of the expiration month.
d. The Chicago Board of Options Exchange is the largest securities market in the United States in terms of the value of traded securities.
e. Each of the above statements is false.

35. Which of the following statements is *false*?

a. Call option values are lower for high-dividend paying stocks.
b. The Option Clearing Corporation steps in every trade and becomes the effective buyer of the option from the writer and the effective writer of the option to the buyer.
c. It is the economic interest of the option buyer to exercise an out-of-the-money call.
d. Option writers are required to post margin amounts to guarantee that they can fulfill their obligations.
e. All of the above statements are false.

36. In the Black-Scholes model, $N(d_1)$ is equal to

   a. the implied volatility of the option.
   b. the present value of the stock's dividend.
   c. the dividend yield of the stock.
   d. the "hedge ratio" for the option.
   e. both b and d

37. In the Black-Scholes model, the option value does not depend on

   a. the risk-free rate of interest.
   b. the exercise price.
   c. the variance of the stock.
   d. the stock price.
   e. the expected rate of return on the stock.

38. In the Black-Scholes model, the value of a call decreases with an increase in

   a. the exercise price.
   b. the stock price.
   c. the time to maturity.
   d. the risk-free rate of interest.
   e. all of the above

39. In the Black-Scholes model, if the standard deviation of the stock increases

   a. the value of a call would increase, but the value of a put would decrease.
   b. both the value of a call and a put would decrease.
   c. the value of a call would increase, but there would be an ambiguous effect on value of a put.
   d. both the value of a call and a put would increase.
   e. the value of a call would decrease but the value of a put would increase.

40. The Black-Scholes option pricing model assumes

   a. investors continuously adjust to a riskless hedge ratio.
   b. all calls are American options.
   c. the variance of the stock is non-constant.
   d. investors are not risk-averse.
   e. only a and b

41.	In the Black-Scholes model, an increase in the market value of the stock will

	a.	increase the value of a call.
	b.	decrease the value of a put.
	c.	increase the value of $N(d_1)$.
	d.	both a and b
	e.	all of the above

SELF-TEST PROBLEMS

1.	Suppose you write a naked call option on Minnesota Mining and Manufacturing stock at a strike price of $100 for a premium of $4.50. What will you gain (or lose) on the call and what will the break-even point be if at option expiration the stock closes at $108?

	a.	$4.50 and $95.50
	b.	-$3.50 and $104.50
	c.	-$8.00 and $104.50
	d.	$4.50 and $104.50
	e.	none of the above

2.	Assume you buy a May 50 put on General Motors for $3.50 when GM is selling at $49 a share. If the stock closes at $50.75 at the expiration date, what will be the value of the put option?

	a.	$3.50
	b.	$0.75
	c.	$2.75
	d.	$1.75
	e.	none of the above

3.	Determine the premium of a bond that is convertible into 20 shares of common stock trading at $45.25 per share. The bond is selling at $1,000 and has a straight debt value of $844.

	a.	$156
	b.	$95
	c.	$61
	d.	$4.75
	e.	none of the above

(The following data apply to Self-Test Problems 4 through 8.)

It is July 1 and UAL stock is at $110. Assume that the stock will pay no dividends between now and the end of November. Premiums for UAL options are as follows:

Stock Price	Strike Price	Calls		Puts	
		Aug.	Nov.	Aug.	Nov.
$110	$105	$8.50	$13.75	$3.00	$6.75
110	110	5.25	10.25	4.75	9.00
110	115	3.50	8.00	7.25	11.75

Jim Smith is considering trading some of the UAL calls if they are properly priced. He asked you to use the Black-Scholes model to calculate the price of UAL calls, given the following information:

Riskless rate = 4 percent (annualized)
Time to expiration for the November option = 142 days
Estimated daily variance of the stock = 0.00040

4. Calculate the Black-Scholes price for the November 110 call. Does your model suggest that the call is undervalued or overvalued?

   a. $10.86, the call is overvalued
   b. $9.71, the call is overvalued
   c. $10.96, the call is undervalued
   d. $11.03, the call is undervalued
   e. none of the above

5. In checking other data, you discover that other traders are using a variance estimate of 0.00034. Recalculate the November 110 call's value using this variance.

   a. $9.75
   b. $10.25
   c. $9.98
   d. $10.86
   e. none of the above

6. Making calculations using the daily variance of 0.0004, the deltas of the November 105 call and the November 115 call are:

    a. .648 and .500
    b. .380 and .002
    c. .591 and .492
    d. .648 and .492
    e. none of the above

7. How many shares of stock would you use to create a riskless arbitrage portfolio for the November 105 call? For the November 115 call?

    a. .648 and .492 shares
    b. 1.54 and 1.93 shares
    c. 1.67 and 2.21 shares
    d. 1.89 and 2.03 shares
    e. none of the above

8. Calculate the Black-Scholes price for the September 110 put.

    a. $9.84
    b. $9.00
    c. $9.26
    d. $10.86
    e. none of the above

ANSWERS TO SELF-TEST QUESTIONS

1.	put		22.	False
2.	European		23.	True
3.	open interest		24.	True
4.	in-the-money		25.	False
5.	Intrinsic value		26.	False
6.	index options		27.	True
7.	time value		28.	True
8.	derivative securities		29.	False
9.	binomial		30.	False
10.	delta		31.	True
11.	callable bond		32.	False
12.	warrant		33.	True
13.	conversion ratio		34.	c
14.	False		35.	c
15.	False		36.	d
16.	True		37.	e
17.	True		38.	a
18.	False		39.	d
19.	True		40.	a
20.	False		41.	e
21.	False			

SOLUTIONS TO SELF-TEST PROBLEMS

1. b.   You have to buy the stock at $108 to deliver and receive the stock price of $100.
         The loss on the call is -$8.00 + $4.50 = -$3.50.
         The break-even point is: $100 + $4.50 = $104.50

2. e.   The value of the put is zero because GM stock price closes above the strike price
         of $50 at the expiration date.

3.   b.   The bond's conversion value is greater than the straight debt value. Therefore, the premium is:

$$\$1{,}000 - (\$45.25)(20) = \$1{,}000 - \$905 = \$95$$

4.   c.   The Black-Scholes equation to calculate call values is:

$$C = N(d_1)S - E(e^{-rt})\,N(d_2)$$

$$d_1 = \frac{\ln(S/E) + (r + \sigma^2/2)T}{\sigma\sqrt{T}}$$

$$d_2 = d_1 - \sigma\sqrt{T}$$

$$d_1 = \frac{\ln(110/110) + (0.04/365 + 0.0004/2)142}{\sqrt{0.0004}\ \sqrt{142}} = \frac{0.0440}{0.2383} = 0.1845$$

$$d_2 = 0.1845 - \sqrt{0.0004}\ \sqrt{142} = -0.0539$$

$$C = N(0.1845)110 - 110(e^{-0.00011(142)})N(-0.0539)$$
$$C = 0.5714(110) - 110(0.9845)(0.4792) = \$10.96$$

The market price is $10.96, suggesting the November 110 call is undervalued.

5.   a.   Using a variance estimate of 0.00034, the November 110 call's value is:

$$d_1 = \frac{\ln(110/110) + (0.04/365 + 0.00034/2)142}{\sqrt{0.00034}\ \sqrt{142}} = \frac{0.0397}{0.2197} = 0.1807$$

$$d_2 = 0.1807 - \sqrt{0.00034}\ \sqrt{142} = -0.0390$$

$$C = N(0.1807)110 - 110(e^{-0.00011(142)})N(-0.0390)$$
$$C = 0.5659(110) - 110(0.9845)(0.4848) = \$9.75$$

6.   d.   The delta of the call is $N(d_1)$, for the November 105 call, the delta is:

$$d_1 = [ln(110/105) + (0.04/365 + 0.0004/2)142]/0.2383 = 0.3797$$
$$N(d_1) = 0.648$$

For the November 115 call, the delta is:

$$d_1 = [ln(110/115) + (0.04/365 + 0.0004/2)142]/0.2383 = -0.0021$$
$$N(d_1) = 0.492$$

7.   e.   For the November 105 call: $1/0.648 = 1.54$ shares per option.
For the November 115 call: $1/0.492 = 2.03$ shares per option.

8.   c.   The Black-Scholes equation to calculate put value is:

$$P = -N(-d_1)S + E(e^{-rt})N(-d_2)$$

For the November 110 put:

$$-d_1 = -0.1845 \text{ (from problem 4)}$$
$$-d_2 = 0.0539 \text{ (from problem 4)}$$
$$P = -0.4286(110) + 110(0.9845)(0.5209) = \$9.26$$

CHAPTER 19

PORTFOLIO MANAGEMENT STRATEGIES USING

PUT AND CALL OPTIONS

OVERVIEW

This chapter describes various option strategies and provides you with a better understanding of the following: (1) put-call parity, (2) theoretical and empirical studies of options, (3) the delta of a portfolio, and (4) straddles, strangles, bull and bear spreads, and butterfly spreads.

OUTLINE

I. Equilibrium relationships between put and call prices—Given the price of either the put or the call, the put-call parity equation shows what the proper price of the other option should be.

$$\text{Put} + \text{Stock} - \text{Call} = \text{Bond}(e^{-rT}) \tag{19.1}$$

II. Portfolio strategies using options.

   A.   Covered call writing—Covered call writing involves selling call options while holding a position in the underlying stock. This is a hedging strategy because the call premium received increases the portfolio's current income and provides some protection against declines in the stock price. However, when the stock appreciates, the covered writer will not share in large gains because the stock will be called away at the exercise price.

   B.   Writing puts and buying Treasury bills—The put-call parity equation shows that the strategy of covered call writing is identical to the sale of puts and buying Treasury bills. This strategy is not popular with institutional investors because when the puts are exercised, the stocks must be purchased when prices are falling.

   C.   Buying protective puts—Buying protective puts involves purchasing puts to hedge against stock declines. This strategy provides a floor on losses and no limit on the gains which can occur.

D. Buying calls and Treasury bills—The put-call parity equation shows that buying protective puts is equivalent to buying a call and investing an amount equal to the discounted exercise price in a Treasury bill. This strategy is called the "90/10" strategy because the call premium is about 10 percent of the fund, leaving 90 percent to be invested in Treasury bills.

E. Studies of option portfolio performance—Covered call portfolios have lower average returns and risks compared to the stock portfolio and the distribution is negatively skewed. The protective put strategy has a higher average return than the covered call writing, but a lower average return than the buy call and Treasury bill strategy.

F. Uses of options by institutional investors—The most popular strategies are protective puts and covered call writing.

III. Managing portfolio risk with options—The difference between using options to change the portfolio's expected return and using the traditional stock/bond weighing scheme is that options produce non-normal return distributions. Options provide patterns of returns that cannot be duplicated at a reasonable cost by traditional ways of combining stocks and bonds in portfolios.

IV. Using delta to measure option portfolio risk—Delta is the change in the option's price for a given change in a stock's price. Delta is only valid for small changes in stock price. The delta of a portfolio consisting of stocks and options is the sum of weighted deltas of all the securities. The delta changes continuously as any of the five factors used in the option pricing model change.

V. Using options to speculate on stock price movements—The leverage and insurance features of puts and calls attract investors who want to speculate on expected price changes of the stock.

A. A straddle is the purchase or sale of a put and call, on the same underlying asset, that have the same contract characteristics. Investors buy a straddle when they expect the stock will move a significant amount, but they do not know in which direction. That is, they expect volatility to increase. A short straddle is the sale of identical puts and calls on the same stock. In stable markets, the sale of a straddle will be profitable, but in volatile markets losses can be substantial.

B. Strangles are identical to straddles except the exercise prices of the put and call are both out-of-the-money. The advantage of the strangle is that it is cheaper than the straddle to implement. Its disadvantage is that the stock has to move more to produce a profit.

C. Bull and bear spreads are positions which include two or more options on the same underlying security that differ only in exercise price. A bull call spread is created by purchasing one call with one strike price and selling another call further out-of-the money. For a bull put spread you sell the higher strike put and buy the lower strike one. A bear put spread is created by buying an at- or near-the-money put and selling one further out-of-the-money. For a bear call spread, you sell the bear strike call and buy one with a higher exercise price.

D. A short butterfly spread is created by purchasing two calls of the same strike, and selling calls with strikes above and below them. Like a long straddle, the short butterfly is used if the trader expects the stock to be volatile. The long butterfly spread is the sale of two at-the-money calls and the purchase of one in-the-money and one out-of-the-money call.

VOCABULARY REVIEW

put-call parity	delta
covered call	straddle
naked call	strangle
writing escrowed puts	bull spread
protective put	bear spread
the 90/10 strategy	butterfly spread
negatively skewed distribution	

SELF-TEST QUESTIONS

Definitional

1. Given the price of either a put or call, the equation which shows what the proper price of the other option should be is called the _____ _____ _____ equation.

2. A conservative strategy of selling calls while holding a position in the underlying stock is called _____ _____ writing.

3. Writing _____ _____ is a strategy involving selling puts and buying Treasury bills.

4. _____ _____ writing is a speculative strategy of selling a call without owning the underlying stock.

5. Buying a _____ _____ is a conservative strategy of purchasing a put while owning the stock to hedge against a possible decline in stock price.

6. The strategy of buying a call and Treasury bills is also called the _____ strategy because the call premium is usually about 10 percent of the value of the investable fund.

7. The change in the option's price for a given change in the price of the stock is called the _____.

8. A _____ is the purchase or sale of a call and a put with the same strike price and time to maturity.

9. A _____ is the purchase or sale of a call and a put with the same time to maturity. However, the strike prices of the call and put are both out-of-the-money.

10. A _____ involves selling an option and buying another option at a different strike price. The option can be a call or a put.

11. Buying one call at a particular strike price and selling another call further out-of-the-money is referred to as the _____ _____ _____ spread because the investor profits from an increase in stock price.

12. A _____ _____ spread is created by purchasing two calls at the same strike price and selling calls with strikes above and below them.

Conceptual

13. Options can be used to increase or reduce portfolio volatility.

    a. True   b. False

14. The distributions created by combining options and other assets are non-normal.

    a. True   b. False

15. Cash dividends cause the value of calls to be higher and puts to be lower.

    a. True   b. False

16. Using the put-call parity relation, if the value of the call is known, the proper value of the put can be determined.

    a. True   b. False

17. The covered call writing strategy is not popular with institutional investors.

    a.   True   b.   False

18. During a period of low volatility, the covered call strategy may produce lower average returns than the portfolio of underlying stocks.

    a.   True   b.   False

19. The strategy of covered call writing is identical to the strategy of writing escrowed puts.

    a.   True   b.   False

20. Buying protective puts produces a return distribution with positive skewness.

    a.   True   b.   False

21. The 90/10 call strategy provides about the same payoffs as the protective put portfolio and is very popular with institutional investors.

    a.   True   b.   False

22. Although the return distributions of option portfolios are non-normal, the traditional mean-variance analysis can still be used to evaluate their performance.

    a.   True   b.   False

23. Delta is valid for small and large changes in the price of the underlying asset.

    a.   True   b.   False

24. The delta of a short-stock position is -1.0.

    a.   True   b.   False

25. The delta of a portfolio is the sum of weighted deltas of all the securities in the portfolio.

    a.   True   b.   False

26. Investors should sell a straddle when they believe the stock will move a significant amount, but they do not know in which direction.

    a.   True   b.   False

27. The advantage of a strangle is that it is cheaper than the straddle to implement.

    a.   True   b.   False

28. A bear spread usually is done using calls because they provide higher payoffs than puts.

    a.   True   b.   False

29. Butterfly spreads are popular with public customers because the payoffs are attractive.

    a.   True   b.   False

30. A protective put is

    a.   a bearish strategy.
    b.   riskier than the strategy of just owning the stock.
    c.   similar to selling a naked put.
    d.   a form of insurance against stock price declines.
    e.   both a and d

31. Which of the following strategies would constitute a riskless investment?

    a.   a bull-call spread
    b.   a short-butterfly spread
    c.   a naked call
    d.   a strangle
    e.   none of the above

32. The change in option's price for a given change in stock price is

    a.   gamma
    b.   delta
    c.   beta
    d.   theta
    e.   none of the above

33. Which of the following strategies would have a negative expected return?

    a.   a 90/10 call strategy
    b.   a bear-put spread
    c.   a butterfly spread
    d.   all of the above
    e.   not enough information to answer

SELF-TEST PROBLEMS

1. Assume you buy 100 shares of a non-dividend paying stock at $53 per share. You hedge by writing a call with an exercise price of $50 and a premium of $5.50. If the stock is selling at $45 at the expiration date of the call, what is the gain or loss of the covered call strategy?

    a. a loss of $8
    b. a loss of $3.50
    c. a gain of $5.50
    d. a loss of $2.50
    e. none of the above

2. Suppose IBM is selling for $51. You buy a May 50 call for $3.50 and write a May 55 call for $1. If IBM closes at $56 at expiration, what will your profit or loss be in the bull call spread?

    a. a $5.00 gain
    b. a $2.50 gain
    c. a $3.50 loss
    d. none of the above
    e. not enough information to answer

3. Assume you sell short 100 shares of Bristol Myers at $68 in May. You buy a July 70 call option for $2.50 to protect yourself from an increase in stock price. If Bristol Myers closes at $80 at the expiration date of the call, what is your gain or loss?

    a. a gain of $7.50
    b. a loss of $2.00
    c. a loss of $4.50
    d. a loss of $12.00
    e. none of the above

(The following data apply to Self-Test Problems 4 through 7.)

Assume that it is April 1 and you are considering how you can profit from Chrysler options. The stock is at $50, the riskless rate is 4 percent (0.0001096 daily), and the variance estimate is 0.0003836 daily. The May expiration date is 46 days away, and the August expiration is 140 days hence.

	Strike Price	Calls		Puts	
		May	August	May	August
		6 1/4	8 3/4	1/4	1 1/2
Delta	45	0.81	0.73	-0.19	-0.27
		2 7/8	5 1/4	2	4 1/2
Delta	50	0.54	0.57	-0.46	-0.43
		1 1/4	3 1/2	6 1/8	8 1/4
Delta	55	0.27	0.40	-0.73	-0.60
		1/2	2 1/8	10 3/8	11 3/4
Delta	60	0.10	0.27	-0.90	-0.73

4.   You currently have a covered call position using the August 50 call. In order to construct a riskless position, what is the appropriate option to add to the covered call position? Are the options properly priced?

a.   Buy the May 50 put. The options are properly priced.
b.   Buy the August 50 put. The options are properly priced.
c.   Sell the August 50 put. The options are overpriced.
d.   Buy the August 60 call. The options are underpriced.
e.   Sell the August 50 put. The options are overpriced.

5.   Consider the following positions: long the stock plus the August 55 put, long the August 60 call plus a Treasury bill. The deltas for these portfolios are

a.   -0.60 and 0.27
b.   1.60 and 0.73
c.   0.40 and 0.27
d.   0.40 and 1.27
e.   none of the above

6. You construct a long-straddle position using August options with a strike price of $50. By how much will this portfolio change in value if the stock goes up $1?

   a. The portfolio value increases $0.14.
   b. The portfolio value decreases $0.14.
   c. The portfolio value remains the same.
   d. The portfolio value increases $0.46
   e. none of the above

7. Assume that you hold 10 May 55 calls. How many May 50 puts should you trade to create a portfolio that is immune to small changes in the price of the stock?

   a. Buy 6.67 May 50 puts.
   b. Sell 10 May 50 puts.
   c. Buy 9.30 May 50 puts.
   d. Sell 9.30 May 50 puts.
   e. none of the above

ANSWERS TO SELF-TEST QUESTIONS

1.	put-call parity		18.	False
2.	covered call		19.	True
3.	escrowed puts		20.	True
4.	Naked call		21.	False
5.	protective put		22.	False
6.	90/10		23.	False
7.	delta		24.	True
8.	straddle		25.	True
9.	strangle		26.	False
10.	spread		27.	True
11.	bull call		28.	False
12.	short butterfly		29.	False
13.	True		30.	d
14.	True		31.	e
15.	False		32.	b
16.	True		33.	e
17.	False			

SOLUTIONS TO SELF-TEST PROBLEMS

1.   d.   The loss of the covered call strategy consists of:
   The loss of the stock position: $45 − $53 = ($8.00)
   The gain of the call premium: $5.50
   Overall loss: ($2.50)

2.   b.   The profit of the bull call spread consists of:
   The gain of the May 50 call: $6 − $3.50 = $2.50
   The gain of the May 55 call: $1 − $1   = $0.00
   Overall gain: 2.50

3.   c.   The overall loss consists of:
   The loss of the stock position: $68 − $80 = ($12.00)
   The gain of the call position: $10 − $2.50 = $ 7.50
   Overall loss: ($ 4.50)

4.   b.   To construct a riskless position, buy the August 50 put. If the options are properly priced, you earn the riskless rate:
$$P + S - C = B(e^{-rt})$$
$$\$4.50 + \$50.00 - \$5.25 = \$50.00[e^{-.04(140/365)}]$$
$$\$49.25 = \$49.24$$
   The options are properly priced.

5.   c.   August 55 put + stock: −0.60 + 1.0 = 0.40
   August 60 call + Treasury bill: 0.27 + 0.0 = 0.27
   The deltas for these positions are 0.40 and 0.27

6.   a.   Buy August 50 call and August 50 put. The delta of the portfolio is: 0.57 + (−0.43) = 0.14. For a $1 change in stock price, the portfolio value increases $0.14

7.   c.   To create a perfect hedge, you want a delta of 0.0
   10 May 55 calls + X May 50 puts = 0.0
   $10(0.40) + X(-0.43) = 0$
   $X = 9.30$
   Thus, buy 9.30 May 50 puts.

CHAPTER 20

FUTURES CONTRACTS: AN INTRODUCTION TO

THEIR MARKETS AND THEIR PRICING

OVERVIEW

This chapter describes a futures contract, the roles of futures markets and gives you a better understanding of the following: (1) the standardized features of a futures contract, (2) domestic and foreign futures markets, (3) the interpretation of futures price quotations, and (4) how futures contracts are priced.

OUTLINE

I. Forward contracts, futures contracts, and their features—A forward contract is an agreement between two parties to deliver a commodity, financial asset, or currency at a future point in time for a price that is agreed on today. A futures contract is a marketable forward contract. Futures contracts are standardized and traded on organized exchanges.

II. Who uses futures markets?

    A. Price discovery—Some people use futures markets to obtain information about the expected future cash price of a commodity.

    B. Hedging—Futures markets can be used by individuals to hedge the price of some commodity that they own or will own at some point in the future.

    C. Speculation—Some people use futures markets to speculate on the price movements of commodities. These speculators accept the price risk that hedgers seek to avoid.

III. Worldwide Exchanges and their futures contracts.

    A. Domestic exchanges—Although an exchange can offer any contract for which it receives permission from the Commodities Futures Trading Commission (CFTC), most exchanges tend to specialize in groups of related products in order to furnish depth to a part of the market. Although most of today's futures volume is found on the Chicago Board of Trade (CBOT) and Chicago Mercantile Exchange

(CME), volume on the New York Mercantile Exchange (NYMEX) has increased steadily in the past few years. Together, these three exchanges and their products compose about 87 percent of the total volume on U.S. futures exchanges.

B. International exchanges—Recently foreign futures exchanges began to generate significant volume when compared to exchanges located in the United States. Even though the CBOT, CME, and NYMEX are the largest in terms of contract volume, six of the next seven exchanges with the largest volume are all foreign.

IV. Futures contracts: their innovation and design.

A. Contract innovation: ingredients for success—When an exchange feels that a new futures contract has the potential to be successful, it writes a proposal outlining its terms and conditions and makes application for the introduction of the new contract to the CFTC. To be approved by the CFTC, the new futures contract must be shown by the exchange to fill an economic need. The qualities that a commodity should possess in order to be considered for a futures contract are: (1) price volatility, (2) competitive market conditions, (3) a large cash market, and (4) a fungible product.

B. Designing futures contracts—Their standardized features. Contracts approved by the CFTC for introduction must have certain standardized terms. Standardized contract terms are one of the features that distinguishes a futures contract from a forward contract. Without standardization it would be very difficult to establish a viable market to trade these contracts.

V. Structure of U.S. Futures Markets.

A. The exchange corporation—Most futures exchanges are nonprofit organizations engaged in the business of trading futures contracts.

B. Exchange members are divided into commission brokers and locals. Commission brokers execute orders for non members. Locals are members who trade for themselves. Locals use three distinct trading strategies: hedging, speculating, and arbitrage. Traders have a variety of trading styles. Scalpers are speculators who attempt to profit from very short-term price movements. Scalpers seldom hold their positions for more than a few minutes. Day traders speculate on intra-day price movements and close out their positions at the end of the day. Position traders maintain long or short positions for weeks or even months. Dual trading is allowed in futures market, meaning that a trader can trade for his own account and act as a broker for a public order as long as the public order is given priority over the private trades.

C.   The clearinghouse—Is a subset of exchange members who guarantee the performance of every trade. The clearinghouse takes the other side of each trade.

VI.   The mechanics of futures trading.

A.   Order placement and operation of the pit—Future orders by individuals are placed through a futures commission merchant (FCM). The order is then sent to the floor of the exchange to the "pit" where the contract is traded.

B.   Margins—The initial margin or a good faith deposit must be posted by both the buyer and the seller at the initiation of the contract to serve as a guarantee of the eventual performance. The amount of initial margin is about 5 percent to 10 percent of the value of the contract. The maintenance margin is a preestablished amount below the initial margin. When the account value falls below this level, the trader receives a margin call and must put additional fund call variation margin to bring the account balance back to its initial margin level.

C.   Daily settlement—Each day gains and losses are credited or debited to both the buyer's and the seller's account by a process known as marking to market.

D.   Daily price limits set the maximum price change in a futures contract relative to the previous day's settlement price. Once a contract hits its limit, trading is still allowed, but at prices bounded by the daily limits.

E.   Closing the futures position—A trader can close out a futures position by an offsetting trade, by mutual delivery, or cash settlement. By far, most futures positions are closed by an offsetting trade, that is, by reversing the position.

VII.   The regulation of futures markets—In addition to the self-regulatory bodies of exchange members such as brokers and exchange clearing house, futures markets are also regulated by the National Futures Association (NFA) and the CFTC.

VIII.   Pricing relationships in futures markets.

A.   The basis is the difference between the cash price and the futures price of a particular contract on the commodity. In a normal market, futures prices increase as the maturity lengthens. In an inverted market, futures prices decline as the contract maturity increases. At maturity, the futures price must converge to be equal to the spot price.

$$\text{Basis} = S_0 - F_{0,t} \tag{20.1}$$

where:

S_0 = spot, or cash, price today ($t = 0$)

$F_{0,t}$ = futures price today ($t = 0$) for delivery at time t.

B. Spreads are the difference between the futures price of one contract and the futures of another contract on the same or different commodity.

$$\text{Spread} = F_{0,t+k} - F_{0,t} \tag{20.2}$$

where

$F_{0,t}$ = futures price today ($t = 0$) for delivery at time t

$F_{0,t+k}$ = futures price today ($t = 0$) for delivery at time $t + k$

IX. Pricing futures contracts—The cost-of-carry model. The futures price of a commodity is the spot price plus the cost of storing the commodity from now until the delivery date.

$$F_{0,t} = S_0(1 + C_{0,t}) \tag{20.3}$$

where

$C_{0,t}$ = percentage cost required to carry or store the commodity from today ($t = 0$) to time t.

A. The cost-of-carry model and the pricing of spreads—According to the cost-of-carry model, the spread between two futures prices should be equal to the cost of carrying the commodity from one delivery date to another:

$$F_{0,t+k} = F_{0,t}(1 + C_{t,t+k}) \tag{20.5}$$

where

$F_{0,t}$ = futures price for the contract expiring at time t

$F_{0,t+k}$ = futures price for a contract expiring at time $t + k$

$C_{t,t+k}$ = percentage cost-of-carry for a commodity from time t to time $t + k$.

B. Market imperfections and the cost-of-carry model—Market imperfections can have an effect on the pricing model. Futures traders are confronted with transaction costs and margin requirements, limitations on short selling, and unequal borrowing and lending rates. These imperfections produce a no-arbitrage trading range or band about the theoretical pricing relationship, so that even though pricing discrepancies may exist, it may be unprofitable for arbitragers to profit from these differentials.

X. Futures prices and expected spot prices.

A. The expectation or risk-neutral theory—Today's futures price should equal the expected spot price at maturity. This theory assumes that futures prices contain no premium to compensate speculators for risk.

$$F_{0,t} = E(S_t) \tag{20.7}$$

B. Normal backwardation theory assumes that futures markets are characterized by short hedgers, forcing speculators to take long positions. Speculators only enter the market if there is a positive expected profit. As a result, futures prices must be less than the expected spot price and will rise over the life of the contract.

$$F_{0,t} < E(S_t) \tag{20.8}$$

C. Contango theory assumes that hedgers hold long positions, on average, forcing speculators to take short positions. Speculators only take price risk if there is a positive expected profit. Therefore, futures prices must be larger than the expected spot price and will decline over the life of the contract.

$$F_{0,t} > E(S_t)$$ (20.9)

D. The capital asset pricing model is the risk premium to be earned by an asset like a futures contract should be related to its beta or systematic risk, not total risk. If a futures contract has zero beta, it should have a zero expected return.

VOCABULARY REVIEW

forward contract
futures contract
price discovery
hedging
spot price
anticipatory hedge
fungible product
tick size
daily price limit
nearby contract
open interest
local
futures commission merchant

scalper
day trader
position trader
dual trading
marking to market
variation margin
basis
inverted market
convergence
cost-of-carry model
normal
normal backwardation market
contango theory

SELF-TEST QUESTIONS

Definitional

1. A non-marketable agreement between two parties to deliver a commodity at a future date for a price that is determined today is called a _____ _____.

2. An investor who is willing to take the price risk of a commodity in the expectation of a profit is called a _____.

3. The minimum price fluctuation of a futures contract is a _____ _____.

4. _____ are exchange members who trade for themselves.

5. Speculators who attempt to profit from very short-term price movements are called _____.

219

6. When an investor receives a margin call, the amount he must deposit to replenish the account and bring it back to the initial margin is called an _____ _____.

7. The _____ is the difference between the cash price of a commodity and the futures price of a particular contract on the commodity.

8. The market where the futures price declines in value as the contract maturity increases is called an _____ market.

9. The difference between futures price of one contract and the futures price of another contract on the same or different commodity is called a _____.

10. The theory which claims that the futures price will always be less than the expected spot price and will rise over the life of the contract is the _____ _____ theory.

Conceptual

11. Futures markets' forecasts are very accurate in determining future spot prices.

    a. True   b. False

12. Futures markets can provide both hedging and speculative opportunities.

    a. True   b. False

13. After a daily price limit is specified in a futures contract, it cannot be changed by the exchange.

    a. True   b. False

14. The futures price of the nearby contract is always less than those of distant contracts.

    a. True   b. False

15. Futures exchanges, such as the Chicago Board of Trade, are non-profit organizations.

    a. True   b. False

16. Locals are exchange members who execute orders for non-members.

    a. True   b. False

17. Position traders are speculators who attempt to profit from very short-term price movements.

    a. True   b. False

18. Dual trading allows a broker to trade for his own account and act as a broker for public orders.

    a. True   b. False

19. The initial margin of a futures contract usually is about five to ten percent of the contract's total value.

    a. True   b. False

20. Most futures positions are closed out by actual delivery or cash settlement.

    a. True   b. False

21. The basis risk is larger than the price risk.

    a. True   b. False

22. In a normal market, futures prices increase as the maturity lengthens.

    a. True   b. False

23. Convergence of cash and futures prices implies that the basis must be equal to zero at maturity.

    a. True   b. False

24. The expectation theory assumes that speculators are risk-neutral.

    a. True   b. False

25. The contango theory is consistent with a negative cost of carry or an inverted market.

   a.   True   b.   False

26. The capital asset pricing model states that positive-beta futures prices should rise.

   a.   True   b.   False

27. Which of the following statements is *most* correct?

   a.   The futures contract is a zero-sum game, losses and gains to all positions netting out to zero.
   b.   Futures markets replace informal forward contracts with highly standardized exchange-traded securities.
   c.   The percentage of futures contracts that result in actual delivery is about 1 percent to 3 percent.
   d.   Both long and short futures traders must post margin.
   e.   All of the above statements are correct.

28. Which of the following is true of a long position in a futures contract?

   a.   It gives you the right to sell an underlying asset at the futures price.
   b.   It obligates you to buy at the futures price.
   c.   It gives you the right to buy an underlying asset at the futures price.
   d.   It obligates you to sell at the futures price.
   e.   either b or d

29. Under conditions of normal backwardation

   a.   the futures price will be greater than the expected spot price.
   b.   the buyer of a futures contract is a hedger.
   c.   the futures price will rise over the life of the contract until the maturity date.
   d.   the seller of a futures contract is a speculator.
   e.   all of the above

30. According to the capital asset pricing model

    a. the futures price is an unbiased estimate of the expected spot price.
    b. if commodity prices have positive systematic risk, futures prices must be lower than expected spot prices.
    c. for any positive-beta asset, the short side of the contract will make an expected profit.
    d. futures prices provide an expected profit of zero to all parties.
    e. futures prices are always lower than expected spot prices.

31. Marking to market is a process associated with a

    a. futures contract.
    b. protective put.
    c. call option.
    d. strip.
    e. forward contract.

32. Which of the following statements is *most* correct?

    a. A futures spread position is riskier than a long position.
    b. The basis risk is larger than the price risk.
    c. Short hedging means protecting the value of an asset by taking a short futures position.
    d. The futures price and spot price must converge at maturity.
    e. Both c and d are correct.

SELF-TEST PROBLEMS

1. You purchase a 5,000-ounce silver futures contract at $3.85 an ounce with an initial margin of ten percent. The price of silver goes to $4.01. What is your rate of return?

    a.   4.16%
    b.   20.78%
    c.   41.56%
    d.   not enough information to answer
    e.   none of the above

2. Suppose you purchase a 5,000-bushel soybean contract for $30,000. The initial margin requirement is $1,100 and the maintenance margin is 75 percent of the initial margin. How much would the price per bushel of soybeans have to fall before you receive a margin call?

    a. $0.055
    b. $0.083
    c. $0.110
    d. $0.275
    e.   none of the above

3. The Kellogg Corporation needs to buy 100,000 bushels of corn in three months to make cereal. The spot price for corn is $2.50 per bushel. A three-month futures contract for corn can be purchased for $2.61. Kellogg wants to hedge by buying 20 futures contracts of corn on the Chicago Board of Trade. If the price of corn is $2.70 in three months, and the futures contracts are closed out at $2.70, what will be the gain (loss) on the futures contract and the net position of Kellogg?

    a. $11,000 and $9,000
    b. $20,000 and −$11,000
    c.   −$9,000 and $11,000
    d. $9,000 and −$11,000
    e.   none of the above

224

(The following data apply to Self-Test Problems 4 through 6.)

GOLD(CMX) 100 troy oz., $ per troy oz.

Delivery Month	Open	High	Low	Settle
August 1993	394.50	394.90	391.50	392.90
October 1993	396.90	396.90	393.80	395.00
December 1993	398.70	399.20	395.50	397.20
February 1994	400.00	400.60	398.40	399.00
April 1994	401.50	401.50	400.50	400.80

Cash price (July 16, 1993) is $392.40

George Graham operates a mine in Arizona that produces gold. He anticipates having about 1,000 troy ounces of gold ready for shipping about December 1, 1993. Today's cash price is $392.40, and George is concerned that gold prices will fall between now (July 16) and December 1.

4. Suppose George decides to hedge his future gold production by using the December 1993 futures contract. Assuming that the settlement price is the relevant futures price, what type of position (long or short) should George take to hedge his production and what will be the gross futures price, in dollars, of his hedge?

    a. short gold futures contracts; the gross futures price is $397,200.
    b. long gold futures contracts; the gross futures price is $397,200.
    c. short gold futures contracts; the gross futures price is $39,870.
    d. long gold futures contracts; the gross futures price is $39,720.
    e. none of the above.

5. Now suppose that December 1, 1993, rolls around and the cash price for gold is 388.50, and the December futures settlement is 390.40. If George decides to offset his futures contract position and deliver his 1,000 troy ounces of gold in the cash market, what is his net gain or loss on his hedge?

    a. net loss of $3,900
    b. net gain of $2,900
    c. net gain of $6,800
    d. net loss of $2,900
    e. none of the above

6. Using the settlement prices for gold, compute the basis for the October futures contract and the spread between the February 94 – April 94 futures contracts.

    a. −$2.60 and $6.60
    b. −$2.60 and $1.80
    c. $2.10 and $1.80
    d. $2.60 and −$1.80
    e. none of the above

ANSWERS TO SELF-TEST QUESTIONS

1.	forward contract		17.	False
2.	speculator		18.	True
3.	tick size		19.	True
4.	Locals		20.	False
5.	scalpers		21.	False
6.	variation margin		22.	True
7.	basis		23.	True
8.	inverted		24.	True
9.	spread		25.	False
10.	normal backwardation		26.	True
11.	False		27.	e
12.	True		28.	b
13.	False		29.	c
14.	False		30.	b
15.	True		31.	a
16.	False		32.	e

SOLUTIONS TO SELF-TEST PROBLEMS

1. c. The value of a silver contract is:
        ($3.85)(5,000) = $19,250
        The initial margin is:
        ($19,250)(10%) = $1,925
        The percentage profit of buying a silver futures contract is:
        [($4.01 − $3.85)(5,000)]/$1,925 = 41.56%

2. a. The maintenance margin is:
75% x $1,100 = $825
The difference between the initial margin and maintenance margin is:
$1,100 − $825 = $275
The amount that can be lost before a margin call is required is $275. The price per bushel of soybeans can fall by:
($275 loss)/5,000 bushels = $0.055 per bushel

3. d. The increase in the price of corn in three months is:
$2.70 − 2.50 = $0.20 per bushel
The overall cost increase to Kellogg is:
$0.20 x 100,000 = $20,000
The overall gain in futures contract is:
($2.70 − $2.61) x (100,000 bushels) = $9,000
The net position of Kellogg is:
$9,000 − $20,000 = −$11,000 (net increase in costs)

4. a. George should short 10 December futures contracts (10 x 100 oz. = 1,000 oz.) to protect his gold production in the event of a decline in the price of gold. The gross futures price of his hedge is (1,000)($397.20) = $397,200.

5. b. George will buy back his ten December futures contracts. His loss in the cash market is ($392.40 − $388.50)(1,000) = −$3,900. His gain in the futures market is ($397.20 − $390.40)(1,000) = $6,800. His net gain is $2,900.

6. b. The basis is the spot price minus the futures price. Thus, the basis for the October futures contract is $392.40 − $395.00 = −$2.60.

The spread between the February 94 − April 94 futures contracts is
$400.80 − $399.00 = $1.80.

CHAPTER 21

PORTFOLIO STRATEGIES USING

FINANCIAL FUTURES

OVERVIEW

This chapter describes various investment strategies using financial futures and gives you a better understanding of the following: (1) hedging strategies, (2) stock index futures, (3) popular interest rate futures, (4) foreign currency futures, and (5) options on futures contracts.

OUTLINE

I.   Hedging concepts—Because there are a limited number of futures contracts available, hedgers must make decisions about which futures contracts to use in their hedging strategies. These include decisions about: (1) which underlying asset to use, (2) the contract maturity, (3) and the hedge ratio, which is the number of futures contracts required to hedge the underlying asset.

    A.   The naive hedging model—The hedger matches the dollar amount of futures contracts to equal the value of the asset to be hedged.

    B.   The regression model—The hedging ratio can be calculated from a regression between the price changes of the two assets. The idea is to minimize the portfolio variance.

$$\frac{W_2}{W_1} = -\frac{\sigma_{12}}{\sigma_2^2} = HR_{r/p} \qquad (21.2)$$

The $HR_{r/p}$ shows the number of futures contracts that should be sold to hedge each long unit of the physical asset.

C. The price sensitivity/duration model is used with assets that are interest rate sensitive. The goal is to create a position in which the unexpected change in value of the cash and the futures contract is zero.

$$HR_{ps} = -\frac{D_s S_0 (1 + r_s)}{D_F F_{0,t} (1 + r_F)} \qquad (21.5)$$

where

HP_{ps} = the number of futures contracts required to hedge the underlying asset
D_s = the duration of the spot instrument
D_F = the duration of the futures contract
S_0 = the current spot price
$F_{0,t}$ = the current futures price
$(1 + r_s)$ = the yield of the cash instrument
$(r + r_F)$ = the yield of the futures.

D. The stock index futures hedging—The hedge ratio used with stock index futures is developed from the regression/portfolio hedge ratio, but the hedge must be calculated using the price changes in the index underlying the futures contract rather than the futures itself. The second modification incorporates the market value of the futures contract so that the appropriate number of futures contracts is determined.

$$\frac{Stock\ index}{contracts} = \frac{V_p}{Index \times Multiplier} \times \beta_{r/p} \qquad (21.6)$$

where
$\beta_{r/p}$ = the hedge ratio
V_p = the value of the stock portfolio.

II. Speculating with futures—By taking a long or a short position in a futures contract, a large profit (or loss) can be earned due to a small initial investment. A spread can be used to reduce the risk in the futures position while still profiting from the investor's belief about the direction of the market.

III. Stock index futures—A stock index futures contract is an agreement to buy or sell a standardized amount of the underlying index at a fixed price on a specified date. Stock index futures are settled in cash rather than by delivery of the underlying index. Prices on stock index futures conform closely to a full cost-of-carry model. If the futures contract is mispriced, a stock index arbitrage will be implemented, creating a riskless hedge that will lock in a profit at maturity from the spot and futures positions.

A. Pricing stock index futures contracts—The equilibrium price for the futures contract, $F_{0,t}$, is the spot value of the index, S_0, continuously compounded from today until the futures expiration, t, by the difference between the riskfree rate, r_f, and the dividend yield, δ, of the index.

$$F_{0,t} = S_0\, e^{(r_f - \delta)t} \qquad (21.7)$$

B. Hedging with stock index futures—A portfolio manager can use a short hedge involving the sale of stock index futures to reduce the risk in the long stock portfolio. On the other hand, a long hedge can be used to gain exposure to equity risk before the cash for investment is received.

C. Portfolio insurance using stock index futures: portfolio managers can use dynamic hedging to create synthetic securities. These managers alter their exposure to stocks by selling or buying stock index futures. If stock prices fall, exposure to stocks is reduced by selling futures.

D. Speculating with stock index futures—The most direct way to speculate with stock index futures is to buy or sell contracts according to your beliefs about the market's future movements. However, these simple trades are very risky because small movements in an index can produce large losses or gains in a futures on the same index or using two different indexes if they believe that segments of the market will behave differently.

IV. Interest rate futures.

A. Treasury bill futures—Each contract calls for delivery at the futures contract expiration of $1,000,000 face value of Treasury bills with 90 days to maturity.

B. Eurodollar futures—The contract uses the add-on yield of the LIBOR (London Interbank Offer Rate) of $1,000,000 face value of Eurodollar deposit. All contracts are settled by cash instead of by physical delivery.

C. Treasury notes and bonds—Treasury note contracts call for delivery of notes with maturity of 2-, 5-, or 10-years, depending on the contract. Treasury bond contracts are settled by delivery of $100,000 U.S. Treasury bond with at least 15 years to maturity or call. Because many Treasury bonds can be used for delivery, their prices must be adjusted by a conversion factor.

D. Hedging with interest rate futures contracts—The purpose of hedging is not to profit from unexpected changes in interest rates, but to remove uncertainty about the value of a financial asset whose future worth is a function of interest rates. For example, a corporate treasurer who will receive a large cash inflow in the near future can buy Treasury bills futures contracts to hedge against a decline in interest rates.

E. Speculating with interest rate futures contracts—Beside hedging, interest rate futures can be used to speculate on the direction of interest rates. Because of the risk in futures positions, most speculators create spread positions. The TED spread (Treasury bills over Eurodollar contracts) is a speculation on nonsynchronous changes in short-term interest rates. The NOB (Treasury notes over Treasury bonds) spread is used to speculate on changes in the level of interest rates or changes in the shape of the yield curve.

V. Futures on foreign exchange.

A. Pricing foreign exchange forward and futures contracts—The short-term relationship between spot and futures prices conforms to a cost-of-carry model called the interest rate parity theorem, which states that differences in the spot and forward rates for currencies are due solely to differentials in interest rates. If futures or forward prices do not conform to the interest rate parity value, a covered interest arbitrage can be used to capture an excess profit.

B. Hedging with foreign exchange futures—Futures on foreign exchange provide a means to hedge foreign exchange rate risk exposure. If an importer of Japanese products believes that yen will appreciate relative to the dollar, he may want to hedge by buying yen contracts in the futures market.

C. Speculating with foreign exchange futures—A trader can speculate on the direction of a foreign currency exchange or bet directly on the price relation among three currencies. The latter is called cross hedging. Because all futures contracts are priced relative to the dollar, it is possible to hedge the exchange rate between two foreign currencies.

VI. Options on futures—The buyer of a call (put) option on a futures contract has the right to take a long (short) position in the underlying futures instrument any time before option expiration. Options on futures are only identical to spot options if they are both European-style, and they expire simultaneously. The Black option on futures pricing model provides theoretically correct prices for European options on forward contracts, but it does not give an exact value for American options on futures. Options on futures can be used to hedge or speculate price risk in the marketplace.

VOCABULARY REVIEW

basis risk	dynamic hedging
hedge ratio	portfolio insurance
naive hedging model	interest rate futures
regression/portfolio model	add-on yield
price sensitivity model	discount yield
spread	conversion factor
intercommodity calendar spread	TED spread
stock index futures	NOB spread
program trading	interest rate parity theorem
stock index arbitrage	covered interest arbitrage
cross hedging	

SELF-TEST QUESTIONS

1. _____ _____ is the uncertainty about changes in the basis of futures and spot prices.

2. The number of futures contracts required to hedge the underlying asset is called the _____ _____.

3. The model which states that the hedger should match the dollar amount of futures contracts to equal the value of the asset to be hedged is called the _____ _____ model.

4. The model which minimizes portfolio variance to determine the hedge ratio is the _____ _____ model.

5. A spread that involves different commodities with the same or different expiration dates is called an _____ _____.

6. _____ _____ refers to the use of computers to monitor continuously the stock and futures prices in order to exploit possible arbitrage opportunities.

7. In Eurodollar futures, the _____ _____ yield is the interest received divided by the amount invested.

8. A spread using Treasury bills and Eurodollar contracts is called the _____ spread.

9. The theorem which claims that differences in the spot and forward rates for currencies are due to differentials in interest rates is called the _____ _____ _____ theorem.

Conceptual

10. The chief determinant of the hedge ratio is the expected relative volatility of the cash asset compared to the expected volatility of the futures position.

    a.   True   b.   False

11. In the regression/portfolio model the hedger matches the amount of futures contracts to the value of the asset to be hedged in order to minimize portfolio variance.

    a.   True   b.   False

12. Because hedging is a risk-reducing activity, hedges are established not to increase return from a position, but to decrease its risk.

    a.   True   b.   False

13. The costs of trading are much lower in the futures markets than in the cash markets.

    a.   True   b.   False

14. A spread that involves the same asset but different expiration dates is called an intercommodity calendar spread.

    a.   True   b.   False

15. Similar to Treasury bond futures, stock index futures are settled by delivery of the underlying asset.

    a.   True   b.   False

16. The most direct way to speculate with stock index futures is to buy or sell contracts, according to your beliefs about the market's direction.

    a.   True   b.   False

17. Both Treasury bill and Eurodollar futures are settled by delivery of the underlying asset.

    a.   True   b.   False

18. The conversion factor system of equating bond values is precise when the term structure is flat.

    a.　　True　　　　　　b.　　False

19. The TED spread is used to speculate on changes in the level of interest rates or changes in the shape of the yield curve.

    a.　　True　　　　　　b.　　False

20. Foreign currency futures and spot prices always conform to the interest rate parity theorem.

    a.　　True　　　　　　b.　　False

21. The benefit to the market of covered interest arbitrage is that it drives spot and forward rates toward their economic value.

    a.　　True　　　　　　b.　　False

22. Options on the spot and options on futures are really identical instruments.

    a.　　True　　　　　　b.　　False

23. Which models are used to determined the hedge ratio for futures?

    a.　　the regression/portfolio model
    b.　　the price-sensitivity/duration model
    c.　　the naive model
    d.　　none of the above
    e.　　all of the above

24. Which of the following statements is *most* correct?

    a.　　Hedges are established to increase returns and to decrease risk from a position.
    b.　　The price-sensitivity/duration model is derived from the idea of minimizing portfolio variance.
    c.　　Most speculators use spreads to reduce the risk in a futures position.
    d.　　All futures contracts are settled by delivery of the underlying asset.
    e.　　All of the above statements are correct.

25. Interest rate futures contracts are available on all of the following *except*

    a. Treasury bonds.
    b. GNMA certificates.
    c. bank certificates of deposit.
    d. Eurodollars.
    e. all of the above

26. While hedging with futures on foreign exchanges reduces the currency risk, it also

    a. maximizes the profit.
    b. eliminates the possibility of a large gain.
    c. has not been popular with corporate managers.
    d. provides an arbitrage opportunity.
    e. none of the above

SELF-TEST PROBLEMS

1. A Treasury bond futures contract with a $100,000 face value is trading at 108–08. What is the dollar value of this futures contract?

    a. $108,080
    b. dependent on its conversion factor
    c. $108,250
    d. $108,500
    e. none of the above

2. A speculator takes a short position in a S&P 500 futures contract at 449.50. The initial margin is $15,000. A month later the futures contract rises to 455.30, and the speculator covers the short position. Assuming no margin cash flows occur during the period, what is the holding period yield?

    a. -19.33%
    b. -29.00%
    c. -3.87%
    d. 19.33%
    e. none of the above

3.   A 90-day Treasury bill futures contract with a delivery value of $1 million is traded on the International Monetary Market at 94.45. What is the price of this Treasury bill futures?

a. $955,500
b. $986,125
c. $944,500
d. $1,000,000
e.   none of the above

4.   The current value of the S&P 500 Index is 430. You want to know the price of a futures contract deliverable in 60 days. The 60-days risk-free interest rate is 1 percent, and the S&P 500 dividend yield is anticipated to be 0.5 percent over the 60-day period. What should be the price of this futures contract?

a.   431.00
b.   430.00
c.   434.30
d.   432.15
e.   none of the above

(The following data apply to Self-Test Problems 5 through 7.)

You are a manager of a $40 million stock portfolio for Fidelity Investments and fear that the market may decline during the next few months. Your portfolio has a beta of 1.1, and you want to hedge its value using S&P 500 Index futures. The multiplier for the contract is $500. The S&P 500 spot index is at 445.75 on July 16 and the December contract is trading for 447.80.

5.   Calculate the number of futures contracts that you must trade to fully hedge you portfolio.

a.   sell 197 contracts
b.   buy 179 contracts
c.   sell 179 contracts
d.   buy 197 contracts
e.   none of the above

6.   Indicate the value of your positions in stock and futures after you create the hedge in July.

a.   long stock of $40 million and short futures of $43.906 million
b.   long stock of $40 million and long futures of $44.108 million
c.   long stock of $40 million and short futures of $44.108 million
d.   short stock of $40 million and long futures of $44.108 million
e.   none of the above

7. Assume it is December 17, the futures' expiration date, and the index has risen to 459.10. You decide to close out your hedge. Your stock portfolio is worth $41,245,310. Calculate the net gain or loss in your total position.

a. net loss of 111,305
b. net gain of 132,260
c. net loss of 132,260
d. net gain of 1,245,310
e. none of the above

ANSWERS TO SELF-TEST QUESTIONS

1.	Basis risk	14.	False
2.	hedge ratio	15.	False
3.	naive hedging	16.	False
4.	regression/portfolio	17.	False
5.	intercommodity calendar	18.	True
6.	Program trading	19.	False
7.	add-on	20.	False
8.	TED	21.	True
9.	interest rate parity	22.	False
10.	True	23.	e
11.	False	24.	c
12.	True	25.	e
13.	True	26.	b

SOLUTIONS TO SELF-TEST PROBLEMS

1. c. The decimal-equivalent of the bond price of 108–08 is: $108 + (8/32) = 1.0825$
The dollar value of the Treasury bond contract is: $\$100,000 \times 1.0825 = \$108,250$

2. a. The loss in the S&P 500 futures contract is:
$(449.50 - 455.30) \times$ (the multiplier of $500) = -\$2,900$
The holding period return is:
$-\$2,900/\$15,000 = -19.33\%$

3. b. The discount yield is:
$100.00 - 94.45 = 5.55\%$ or 0.0555
The price of the 90-day Treasury bill futures contract is:
$\$1,000,000 \times [1 -(\text{discount yield} \times (90 \text{ days}/360 \text{ days}))]$
$= \$1,000,000 \times [1 - (.0555 \times 90/360)] = \$986,125$

4.   d.   The cost-of carry equation for stock index futures is:

$$F_{0,t} = S_0 e^{(r-\delta)t}$$

$$
\begin{aligned}
F_{0,t} &= (430)e^{[(.01-.005)/60\ \text{days}]60\ \text{days}} \\
&= 430e^{.005} \\
&= 430(1.0050) \\
&= 432.15
\end{aligned}
$$

5.   a.   The hedge ratio is:

$HR = [(V_p)/(\text{Index})(\text{Multiplier})] \times \beta_{r/p}$

$\quad\quad = [\$40,000,000/(447.80)(\$500)] \times 1.1 = 196.52$

You should sell 197 contracts.

6.   c.   Your position in July is:

Value of long stock $40,000,000

Short December futures (197 x 447.8 x 500) = 44,108,300

7.   b.   The value of 197 futures contracts on September 20 is:

$\quad\quad$ 197(459.10)($500) = $45,221,350

The portfolio value is $41,145,310

The increase in stock value is:

$\quad\quad$ $41,245,310 - $40,000,000 = $1,245,310

The loss in futures contracts is:

$\quad\quad$ $44,108,300 - $45,221,350 = -$1,113,050

The net gain from hedge is:

$\quad\quad$ $1,245,310 - $1,113,050 = $132,260

CHAPTER 22

PERSONAL PORTFOLIO MANAGEMENT:

A SUGGESTED GUIDELINE

OVERVIEW

This chapter illustrates the following: (1) why it is important for an investor to establish a financial goal, (2) why a systematic plan of saving and investing is crucial in attaining financial goals, (3) why it is important to control for the effects of taxes in inflation, and (4) how diversification and asset allocation can be useful in controlling for risk without sacrificing a lot of return.

OUTLINE

I.   Establish your long-term financial goal—The first step toward successful investing is to set a long-term financial goal.

II.   Develop a financial plan to meet your financial goal—A financial plan is a systematic plan of investing to accomplish the objective of accumulating a set amount of money. Developing a financial plan involves budgeting.

III.   Evaluate the consequences of contingencies to your long-run goal and financial plan—The next step is to conduct a review of any contingencies that may preclude the achievement of the financial goal. Contingencies include problems that might arise because of poor health, disability, or death. Make sure you have adequate health insurance, disability insurance, and life insurance.

IV.   Building a portfolio to meet your financial goal.

        A.   Personal versus professional management—You must decide whether to manage the portfolio yourself or hire a professional money manager to do it for you. If you choose to use the service of a professional, you can select a mutual fund or a private money manager. Mutual funds are suitable choices for investors with a limited amount of money to invest, whereas private money managers are better suited for wealthier investors.

B.   Determine your personal preferences for risk and expected return—Depending on your preferences, you have a broad array of investment choices, potential returns, and risks. There is a steady increase in risk and average return as you move from short-term money market instruments such as Treasury bills to bonds to common stocks. The choice of securities depends on your personal preferences.

C.   Establish portfolio objectives and construct a diversified portfolio to meet those objectives—Common portfolio objectives are growth, income, preservation of capital, balanced, or some combination of them. Pay attention to asset allocation decisions which determine the proportion of investment in stocks, bonds, and money market securities. For a long-term investor, asset allocation is far more important than market timing and security selection.

D.   Set a time for periodic review and evaluation—Generally, reviews are needed every year to assess the reliability of the budget estimates, the performance of the portfolio, and possible changes in personal objectives.

VOCABULARY REVIEW

financial goal	asset allocation
financial plan	term insurance
contingency	market timing
dollar-cost averaging	timing risk
value averaging	

SELF-TEST QUESTIONS

Definitional

1.   A systematic plan of investing to accumulate a set amount of money is called a _____ _____ .

2.   A technique which allows you to invest a fixed amount of money every month is called _____ _____ _____ .

3.   _____ averaging forces you to make extra investment in a month when stocks are down and to invest less when stocks advance.

4.   A _____ account pays a flat fee of about 3 percent annually which includes all transaction costs and management fee.

5.   _____ _____ determines the amount you invest in each asset category, such as stocks and bonds.

6. The risk of liquidating the portfolio at a time when the market is down is called the
_____ _____.

Conceptual

7. Most financial goals are oriented to the short-term.

   a. True   b. False

8. In the United States, less than 5 percent of the population can support themselves financially when they retire.

   a. True   b. False

9. Private money managers are suitable choices for investors who have a limited amount of money to invest.

   a. True   b. False

10. Dollar-cost averaging strategy is less risky than the buy-and-hold strategy.

    a. True   b. False

11. A growth portfolio is suitable for investors with a low tolerance for risk.

    a. True   b. False

12. In the long run, market timing is more important than asset allocation in determining the portfolio performance.

    a. True   b. False

13. Diversification can reduce the risk of the portfolio without affecting the expected return.

    a. True   b. False

14. Advantages of mutual funds include

    a. outperforming the stock market on average.
    b. efficient diversification.
    c. individual attention.
    d. exceptionally low risk.
    e. all of the above

15. By using dollar-cost averaging

    a. the investor attempts to beat the market.
    b. the investor applies the market timing strategy.
    c. the investor invests a fixed amount at regular intervals.
    d. the investor buys when stock prices are favorable only.
    e. none of the above

16. Which funds invest primarily in short-term securities, usually with maturities of 90 days or less?

    a. asset allocation funds
    b. balanced funds
    c. index funds
    d. money market funds
    e. none of the above

ANSWERS TO SELF-TEST QUESTIONS

1.	financial plan		9.	False
2.	dollar-cost averaging		10.	True
3.	Value		11.	False
4.	wrap		12.	False
5.	Asset allocation		13.	True
6.	timing risk		14.	b
7.	False		15.	c
8.	True		16.	d